The Women and Children
of the Alamo

Acknowledgements

My deepest appreciation goes to the people who shared their expertise with me while I researched and wrote *The Women and Children of the Alamo*.

The special librarians and archivists at the University of Texas at Austin were invaluable in my research and in helping me locate the answers to innumerable questions on Texas and Mexican history: Mary Beth Fleischer, Trudy Croes, Ralph Elder and Bill Richter of the Barker Texas History Center; and Wanda Turnley and Jane Garner of the Benson Latin American Collection Library. Several staff members of the State Archives devoted time in guiding me in my quest for old documents. Dr. James Brown discussed with me aspects of Mexican army firearms of the 1830s.

In San Antonio my work was enriched by suggestions from Marie Berry, research director of the San Antonio Public Library. Sharing their knowledge with me in my search for pictures were Wallace Saage, director of the Alamo Curator's Library, and Martha Utterback, of the Daughters of the Republic of Texas Library at the Alamo, who helped me find old San Antonio pictures and assisted me with the Theodore Gentilz and the Morgan Wolfe Merrick collections. Special thanks go to John Ogden Leal for his translations of civil and church records of San Antonio de Béxar, which are deposited in the Daughters of the Republic of Texas Library at the Alamo. The helpfulness of the entire Alamo Library staff was a continuing source of encouragement during my research.

Of the often-called-upon family and friends, I remember: Etna Rhoades Scott for the generous sharing of her research on the Losoya and Esparza families; Juana Navarro Alsbury's San Antonio descendants Gilbert

The 1849 Daguerreotype of the Alamo

The earliest datable photograph taken in Texas, and the only extant photograph of the Alamo prior to the construction in 1850 of the now familiar façade. Courtesy The Briscoe Papers of The Center for American History of The University of Texas at Austin.

The Women and Children of the Alamo

by Crystal Sasse Ragsdale

&

State House Press

1994

Library of Congress Cataloging-in-Publication Data

Ragsdale, Crystal Sasse.
The women and children of the Alamo / by
Crystal Sasse Ragsdale.
p.   cm.
Includes bibliographical references.
ISBN 1-880510-11-1 — ISBN 1-880510-12-X (pbk.)
ISBN 1-880510-13-8 (signed limited)
1. Alamo (San Antonio, Tex.)—Siege, 1836—Biography.
2. Women—Texas—San Antonio—Biography.
3. Children—Texas—San Antonio—Biography.
4. San Antonio (Tex.)—Biography.
[1. Alamo (San Antonio, Tex.) — Siege, 1836 — Biography.]
I. Title.

F390.R115   1994   93-41998
976.4'03'082—dc20

Printed in the United States of America

Second Printing

*Cover illustration: Detail of original 1901 painting by
Verner Moore White. Courtesy The Alamo Curator*

State House Press
P.O. Box 15247
Austin, Texas 78761

In Memory
of

the spirited women of San Antonio de Béxar
who endured all manner of dangers
—epidemics—droughts—floods—wars—

and of

Bernice Rhoades Strong,
archivist of the
Daughters of the Republic of Texas Library
at the Alamo

કે

Table of Contents

Patiño, Jr. and George N. Pérez for their stories of that gracious lady; Christopher W. Williams for his patient counseling on computer intricacies; kinswomen Thelma Wallace Glaze who demanded that structural sense accompany historical statement, and E'Lane Carlisle Murray who emphasized the need for clear meanings; Paul C. Ragsdale who shared his knowledge of the Siege and Storming of Béxar and of the people, places and maps of Texas; and editor Erik J. Mason for his gracious patience and masterly guidance in the evolvement of the manuscript.

During quiet reflections in the carefully tended Alamo grounds under the shade of its trees and among the flowers bordering the remnant of the old *acequia*, I found the imaginative, motivating and inspiring link I sought with the past of the old Alamo.

CSR
Austin, August 1993

Glossary

ACEQUIA, irrigation canal or ditch.

ACEQUIA MADRE, "mother" or main irrigation channel from which feeder canals run. The Alamo's *Acequia Madre* curved eastward just behind the Alamo chapel then branched to run alongside Alamo Plaza before flowing on to the other missions and farm fields six miles to the south.

ÁLAMO, cottonwood tree. The name by which the San Antonio de Valero mission and presidio came to be known in the early 1800s.

ALCALDE, elected, "literate" citizen of a Mexican *villa* whose duties were similar to those of a mayor and justice of the peace. He carried a silver-headed cane as a sign of office and at times, if he could not be present at an official occasion, sent his cane to represent him.

BEJAREÑO/A, man or woman resident of San Antonio de Béxar.

CAMINO REAL, King's Highway, Old San Antonio Road. Blazed in 1691 by first provincial governor of Texas, as the route from Presidio del Rio Grande (below present-day Eagle Pass) to the missions in Texas.

CAMPO SANTO, sanctified ground. A cemetery set aside for burying members of the Roman Catholic church.

CUARTELES/QUARTELES, barracks, military quarters. *Cuarteles del Álamo* were the barracks at the Alamo; others were at Military Plaza or in the nearby *La Villita* area.

CUBA LIBRE MOVEMENT, political activism in the United States supporting the Cuban revolutionists' movement for independence against Spain at the end of the nineteenth century.

DEGÜELLO, attack without quarter. At the attack signal against the Alamo on the morning of the sixth of March, 1836, Mexican army bands played the historic battle chant ordering complete destruction of the enemy without mercy.

EMPRESARIO, title given to a developer or colonizer who received large land grants in Spanish and Mexican Texas for the express purpose of bringing immigrants to settle the vast, unoccupied areas.

ESCOPETA, musket, Brown Bess. A short, wide-barreled shotgun of uncertain dependability and limited firing range. These

European-made guns were imports into Mexico during the Texas Revolution. The *escopeta* with bayonet attached became a formidable weapon for the inexperienced Mexican militia in hand-to-hand combat against the Texans, who could only use their more acccurate, long range Tennessee rifles as clubs when they ran out of powder.

FANDANGO, name of a Spanish dance. In Texas a *fandango* came to designate a gathering place in the evening where men might meet and dance with young women in a chaparoned atmosphere.

HERMANO/A, brother or sister. The terms are often used as an affectionate, familiar form of address.

JACAL (ES), small, fragile dwelling constructed of tree limbs and branches, with a roof of *tules* (cattail leaves) or grass. A simple place to sleep and to escape rain, cold or heat.

LA VILLITA, village. A well established area of San Antonio de Béxar, southwest of the Alamo, where soldiers and their families lived during Spanish and Mexican control of Texas.

LA PLAZA DE LAS ISLAS, Principal or Main Plaza. Important central area of town officially designated for civilian uses. It was named for the Canary Island settlers who arrived in San Antonio de Béxar in 1731. Authorities laid out the plaza according to ancient Spanish colonial laws. On the west it was bounded by San Fernando church on San Pedro Creek. On the other three sides were various government, commercial and residential buildings. Its name has changed through the years; in the early 1980s the original designation was re-affirmed as La Plaza de las Islas.

LA PLAZA DE LAS ARMAS, Military Plaza. This plaza lies immediately west of the San Fernando Cathedral. For decades it was enclosed by Spanish then Mexican military headquarters and barracks. After Texas independence it became a major freighting yard for wagons and ox carts bringing in merchandise from Mexico and for the reloading of goods for northern Mexico and West Texas.

MADRINA, godmother. Woman religious sponsor during baptismal and wedding ceremonies.

MANO, hand. Smooth stone tool used with a *metate* as a rolling pin in grinding the softened, shelled corn into the flour used in *masa,*the dough for *tortillas.*

MANTILLA, light weight, silk lace shawl worn over the head at formal ceremonies, church, and social occasions. It is usually draped over a tall, decorated comb placed at the back of the head and falls over the shoulders in graceful folds.

METATE, sturdy, grey stone, miniature table. A culinary necessity of the Mexican kitchen. Women knelt on the floor above it pushing the *mano* back and forth over the water-softened kernels of corn. The process is painstakingly illustrated by Theodore Gentilz in his painting, "La Cocina."

PADRINO, godfather. Male counterpart of a *madrina*.

QUIEN SABE? Who knows? Often said with an accompanying gesture of questioning; used as a final phrase to an unanswerable question.

REBOZO, wide, fringed shawl. Woven of cotton, wool or silk, they are made in varying lengths. Of *mestizo* (Mexican and Indian) origin, they were worn by all classes of Mexican women beginning in the sixteenth century. *Rebozos* were used to carry babies and other items in the voluminous folds. It is said that for the Mexican woman "the *rebozo* is like her flag—it serves as her cradle, her shelter, her protection and even her shroud."

SOLDADERAS, women who accompanied Mexican armies. Following the soldiers on the march, they brought their babies and children with them. *Soldaderas* were wives and sweethearts, and camp followers, who cooked for the soldiers, did their laundry, and at times were their nurses. The women and children's presence during times of battle often caused divided loyalties for the soldiers concerned for their family's safety.

SEÑOR/SEÑORA, Mr./Mrs.

SERAPE, colorful, cotton or wool blanket often centered with a quadrangular figure. This garment, worn by all classes of Mexican men, goes back to the Mexoamerican, pre-Columbian epoch. It is used "as a coat, a bed, and sheltering roof, a cloak for hiding, a shield for fighting and more importantly, a status symbol for both weaver and wearer."

TEJANO/A, Texas Mexicans. Most *Tejanos* were loyal to the Texas side during the revolution against Mexico. Despite their good faith and invaluable services during those years, their interests were often rudely ignored by new arrivals to Texas following independence.

TÍO/TÍA, uncle/aunt.

VILLA, small town.

VIRGIN DE GUADALUPE, *Nuestra Señora de Guadalupe*, "Mother of God, Mother of the Americas." Her picture is possibly the most widely known image in Mexico. The dark-skinned virgin appeared to Indian Juan Diego in 1531 on an ancient temple site near Mexico City and left her likeness imprinted on his *tilma* or cape. Within a short time, she became the newly conquered Indians' guardian and protector. Named after the Spanish *Nuestra Señora de Guadalupe de Estremadura*, she is unlike her counterpart for she does not have the Christ child with her nor is she clothed in a stiff formal dress. It was no accident that Father Miguel Hidalgo y Costilla chose to place the popular icon on his standard for the Mexican War of Independence against Spain in 1810.

map by Charles Shaw

LORE AND LEGENDS

❧

Anyone familiar with the history of Texas knows the epic saga of the siege and fall of the Alamo. The riveting story ends in tragedy with 189 of the brave defenders of the fort lying dead. But there were others who *did* survive the final massacre within the broken walls of the ruined mission—several men who passed into history with their tales untold and, more importantly, those of the more than a dozen women and children who both survived the ordeal and who later recounted the thrilling tales of their experiences.

For thirteen days in 1836, from Tuesday, February 23 to Sunday, March 6, Texans and *tejanos* (Mexican Texans loyal to the cause of Texas freedom) remained trapped in the Alamo while Mexican forces surrounded the mission-fortress. At dawn of the final day thousands of Mexican soldiers overran the Alamo and left the defenders lying dead in the ruins after a half-hour of intense assault and fighting.

The siege began at noon on February 23 when Mexican General Antonio López de Santa Anna captured the old military and civilian outpost town of San Antonio de Béxar. In frenzied confusion a crowd of Alamo soldiers and local citizens—men, women, and children—fled helter-skelter into the fort. Within a short time several of the terrified citizens changed their minds and decided not to remain within the Alamo walls. Since the men of these families—Menchaca, Flores, Rodríguez, Ramírez, Arocha, and Silvero—were not soldiers, Santa Anna allowed them to escort their wives and children away from town to distant ranches. Alamo commander William

THE ALAMO
1836

ACEQUIA
OF THE ALAMO

DRY ACEQUIA

OFFICERS' QUARTE[...]

PECAN TREE

BEXAR (800 YARDS)

drawing by Charles Shaw

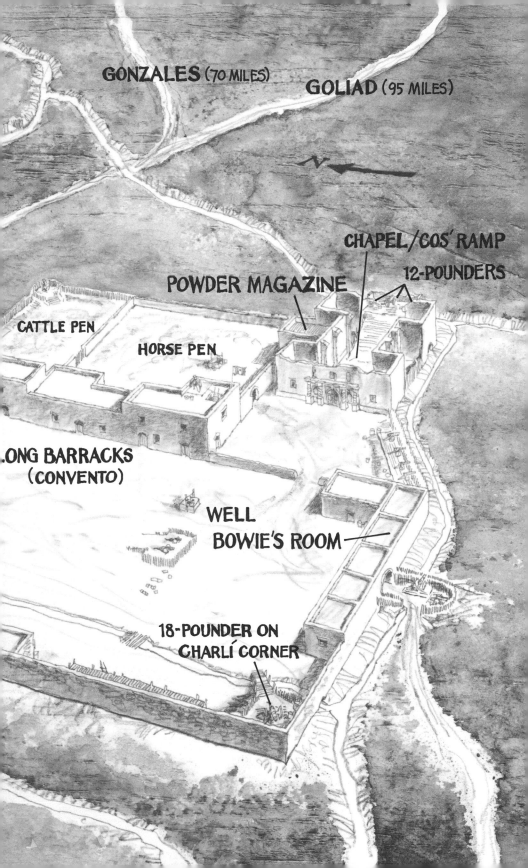

GONZALES (70 MILES)

GOLIAD (95 MILES)

N

CHAPEL/COS' RAMP

12-POUNDERS

POWDER MAGAZINE

CATTLE PEN

HORSE PEN

LONG BARRACKS
(CONVENTO)

WELL

BOWIE'S ROOM

18-POUNDER ON
CHARLÍ CORNER

Barret Travis resented their leaving, although their number would soon have become a severe burden on the Alamo's limited food supply. Even though these families left, a number of refugees remained.

They were women and children, a dozen or so of them in addition to several black men who were servants of Bowie and Travis. No one knows to this day just how many nor who they all were. What we *do* know of their lives in the Alamo during the thirteen days of the siege and final storming came not from their own writings—all of them were illiterate except for Juana Navarro Pérez Alsbury—but from interviews. Journalists listened to their remembrances, but in writing them down often interpreted and rephrased the speakers' words. Other even less viable reports of their ordeals were based not on the actual first-hand accounts but, rather, on the writers' opinions founded sometimes on hearsay and misinformation. All the interviews and accounts, however, usually begin as Santa Anna's armies entered San Antonio de Béxar on that February day.

Where did they hide, these civilians who stayed behind? The safest places for them at first were within the thick-walled rooms of the church and in the officers' quarters in the northwest corner of the plaza quadrangle. The small room just to the right of the entrance of the church became the ultimate refuge for most of the women and children during the last battle.

Two of the women with their children, the families of artillery commander Almaron Dickinson and his artilleryman Gregorio Esparza, took refuge in locations their husbands chose for them just below the gun emplacements at the east end of the church. Susanna Dickinson with her baby Angelina were joined by Ana Esparza with her family, which included María, her daughter by her first marriage, eight-year-old Enrique (over the years sometimes described as twelve), who was later to tell of his Alamo experience, and his two younger brothers Manuel and Francisco.

Since artillery gunner Anthony Wolfe (also spelled Wolf) was also at the artillery post with Dickinson and

Esparza, it seems likely that his twelve and eight-year-old sons stayed with the Esparza family. Although Anthony Wolfe is listed among the Alamo dead, many details regarding him and his sons remain an unsolved mystery.

Enrique Esparza also recalled six other *tejanas* who shared the Alamo's protection—Petra Gonzales, known as Nena, was an "old woman," but Trinidad Saucedo was a "beautiful, young girl." She is possibly the one listed in 1830 as a member of Erasmo Seguín's household in the San Antonio de Béxar census for the *Barrio del Sur.* Enrique also remembered that a *Señora* Vitono de Saline and her three daughters hid with them within the church. Unfortunately, after the battle these six women and children disappear into unrecorded history.

Other *tejanas* were aristocrats Juana Navarro Pérez Alsbury (sister-in-law of James Bowie) with her baby son, Alejo Pérez, and her younger sister Gertrudis Navarro. Years later, San Antonio artist Theodore Gentilz noted in his research that a young servant girl, Antonia Fuentes, accompanied Juana Alsbury to the Alamo that frightful afternoon.

Tejana Concepción Charlí Gortari Losoya fled into the Alamo with her grown daughter Juana and young son Juan. Her older son Toribio was already there as one of the Alamo's *tejano* defenders.

Madame Candelaria is one of the best-known for her Alamo remembrances, although some of her contemporaries as well as some modern revisionists dispute her presence in the Alamo. Decades after the battle a group of San Antonio citizens twice requested the Texas legislature to award Madame Candelaria a pension for her faithful services during the Alamo conflict. Finally, in the early 1890s, she was granted a monthly pension of twelve dollars in recognition of both her nursing care during a yellow fever epidemic in San Antonio and "for her service to the wounded and sick during the Siege of 1836." Despite the controversy over her presence in the Alamo, she remained a living monument to the past and continued to tell the dramatic Alamo story throughout her long life.

Sharing the fear and terror in the Alamo were several black men and possibly several black women. Sam, one of Bowie's slaves, is sometimes reported to have been in the Alamo. Far better known is Joe, Travis's black slave and aide-de-camp, who gave vivid reports of the battle and was much quoted. He told of one young, black woman among them who was killed when she dashed into cannon fire "while attempting to cross the Alamo [plaza]. She was found lying between two guns." Another black woman, a servant, is known to have accompanied the Navarro sisters to their father's home after the battle.

Two of the women survivors—Susanna Dickinson and Madame Candelaria—later told and retold their stories. Juana Alsbury, however, spoke little English, and after her initial interviews with her friends Mary Maverick and John S. Ford, was seldom quoted regarding her Alamo experiences. Enrique Esparza, as an old man in the early twentieth century, gave several versions of his childhood adventures during the frightening days and nights within the Alamo.

There were few similarities in the lives of the women who fled their homes in Béxar and raced to the Alamo that February day, yet from that first afternoon until after their interview with Santa Anna following the battle, they shared a common experience. Each reacted to the same tragic drama in her own way. Their varied recollections are told in this book.

If their memories seemed faulty and confused through the passing years—if their stories varied from telling to telling—who can fault them? They survived to provide history with narratives of what life was like inside the Alamo through the last fatal day of March 6, 1836.

THE ALAMO AND ITS HISTORY

༺⁂༻

The buildings and plaza where a handful of Texans and *tejanos* died fighting against the overwhelming forces of the Mexican army on March 6, 1836, is known today as the Alamo, although this name, from the Spanish word *álamo* for cottonwood tree, did not come into use until the early 1800s. The original mission, known as San Antonio de Valero, was founded in 1718, the oldest of the five Spanish missions of the *villa* San Antonio de Béxar. For almost a hundred years the mission's name on maps and official documents remained San Antonio de Valero, in both religious reverence for Saint Anthony of Padua and in political recognition of the Marqués de Valero, a Spanish viceroy to Mexico.

The exact site of the original mission remains in dispute after all these years, one of the many several-centuries-old mysteries which shroud the long-forgotten facts with unanswered questions and intriguing legends. This first site in 1718 was a cluster of huts located somewhere on the east bank of the San Antonio River, possibly near *Plaza de las Armas* (Military Plaza). The site for the mission, however, was to change at least twice, and within a short time a second mission rose to replace the first, south of the present Alamo, perhaps near Saint Joseph's Church on present day East Commerce Street. Not until a "furious hurricane" scattered this second mission's structures in 1724, could a third site claim permanent buildings. Priests blessed the new grounds on a rise of land overlooking the river east of the village San Antonio de Béxar. This time Franciscan priests built with enduring quarried limestone, adobe and wooden timbers.

The mission was established for the Indians of Texas. A school soon opened to educate these new Christians, to teach them the ways and beliefs of the Spanish, and to train them in trades and farming. As time went on the size of the mission complex grew. Within a high, stone-walled plaza the priests occupied their headquarters just northwest of the Alamo church. This two story *convento* housed their living quarters, dining rooms, kitchen, and offices.

Through the years uses for various rooms changed or additional ones were built as the need arose. Storerooms protected bags of cotton and wool. In workshops stood wheels for spinning thread and looms for weaving. From the fabrics women stitched clothing for the colony of mission Indians. The men worked in the blacksmith shop and in the pottery and tile factory. The Indians who lived at the mission brought the harvests of beans and corn, cultivated on the mission's farm lands, to a solid-wall granary maintained in the south section of the Alamo compound wall. Part of this granary later became known as the "low barracks" when the buildings were taken over by the Spanish military in the early nineteenth century. The walls of the present Alamo church building still reveal various old openings filled in through the years to meet new uses.

Several settlements clustered along the walls of the plaza. Inside, the Indians lived across from the *convento* in rooms built into the protecting west walls of the plaza. *Jacales,* small brush huts, were attached to the outside of the south walls as living quarters for employees at the mission; later soldiers and their families made their homes here.

On mission lands to the southwest in nearby *La Villita* lived other families, quite apart from San Antonio de Béxar but whose members attended church at the Alamo. Sixteen families of colonists from the Canary Islands settled in Béxar in 1731, establishing their own site just east of Military Plaza and calling it *villa* San Fernando de Béxar. Soon they built San Fernando church facing *La Plaza de las Islas* and clustered their

San Fernando Church in Main Plaza. An 1837 sketch by George Ware Fulton. Courtesy The Center for American History of The University of Texas at Austin.

homes about the plaza in an enclave of their own making. In time *bejareños* shortened the name to *Plaza Principal*, and during the period of the Republic of Texas this historic center became known as Main Plaza.

The first church on the third and final site of the mission de Valero was not completed until about 1744 and lasted perhaps ten years. When the tower and sacristy of this structure collapsed, the priests reconstructed the second and present church in 1758—the date still stands above the door in the carved stone façade. But once again the superstructure—the tower, dome, and arched roof—collapsed. Only the walls along each side with the sacristy, baptistry, confessional and other small rooms remained standing, and so the building was to remain.

Perhaps the building problems of the falling roof and collapsing dome were simply that the local workmen did not have the skills to carry out the priests' plans for such

Architectural Detail of Alamo façade drawn in 1961 by W. Eugene George, Jr. for the Historic American Buildings Survey. Images of Saints Francis and Dominic originally filled the lower two niches. Courtesy Daughters of the Republic of Texas Library at the Alamo.

grand architecture. Other projects failed as well. Hopes of Christianizing the Indians fell away as epidemics reduced the number of converts living at the mission. Runaways returned to their old customs of living, further diminishing the number of native inhabitants.

Church authorities finally ordered the priests to give up their work at mission San Antonio de Valero, and in 1793 the Spanish government took over control of mission properties in Texas. Local Indians and bejareños encroached upon the lands and outbuildings of the mission compound. During these years of neglect, as

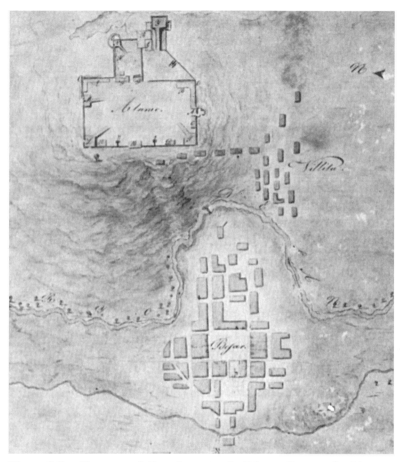

Plan of the Alamo and San Antonio de Béxar. Drawn for Vicente Filisola in March 1836 shortly before the Mexican attack. Courtesy The Center for American History of The University of Texas at Austin.

mission walls crumbled, the townspeople hauled off stone and timbers for their own houses. Even carved stone pieces were taken away to become part of other missions along the San Antonio River.

Yet the strategic importance of the mission remained, even in its dilapidated condition, and in the early nine-teenth century around 1803 occurred both a revival of life around the old buildings and a new name. A Spanish cavalry unit arrived from the northern Mexican town of Parras to take up their new military station, bringing with

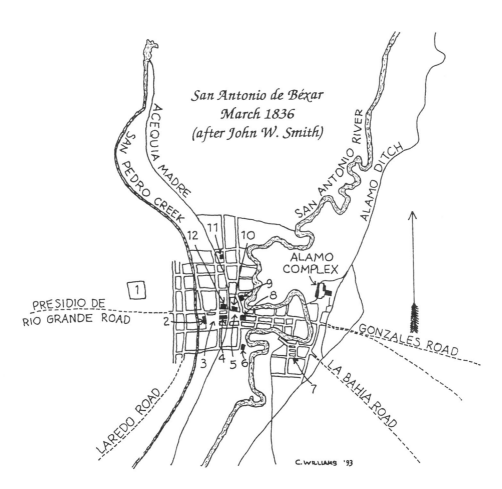

1. Campo Santo
2. Governor's Palace
3. Military Plaza
4. San Fernando Church
5. Main Plaza
6. La Quinta (House)
7. La Villita
8. Músquiz House
9. Veramendi Palace
10. Iturri House (Santa Anna's Headquarters)
11. Esparza House
12. Navarro House

San Antonio de Bejar in 1835. Adapted by Christopher Williams from the 1835 map by John W. Smith in the Martin L. Crimmins Papers in the Daughters of the Republic of Texas Library at the Alamo.

them their name *San José y Santiago del Álamo*. The full title was shortened to *Álamo* at their headquarters and the new appellation soon replaced the older name of San Antonio de Valero. Soldiers' barracks quickly supplanted the Indian quarters along the plaza's western and southern walls.

For a number of years after their arrival, the cavalry was used primarily to fight off Indian raids. In 1811 and 1813 Spanish soldiers used the Alamo as a fortress against the rebels during Mexico's war against Spain's control. After Mexican independence in 1821, the Spanish forces departed and fourteen years passed before any sizeable military forces again occupied the ragged but durable mission-turned-fortress.

By 1835 another revolution was in the making— Texans and *tejanos* demanded more self-government from Mexico. In answer to their rumblings dictator Santa Anna dispatched General Martín Perfecto de Cós with an army to establish firmer control over Texas. Cós arrived in San Antonio in October 1835, set up his military headquarters, and began repairing the Alamo's walls, buildings, and artillery emplacements. Below the yawning gap in the church roof he constructed a ramp, rising from near the front entrance back to the east wall, to reach a battlement for three cannon facing east, south, and north.

Cós never completed his repairs. In early December the Texans and *tejanos* initiated an attack on the Mexican army in Béxar and, after intense fighting, Cós sent a white flag of surrender in the early morning of December 9. The victors permitted the Mexican commander to return with his army to Mexico. Before leaving, however, Cós committed one final act of revenge upon the Texas rebels.

He left the Alamo a ruin. By ordering the destruction of much of his repair work, the defeated general made certain the battle prize would be but a shell of a fortress. Wide gaps in the outer protecting walls as well as broken interior stone walls would take months to reset even partially.

During the following month of January and three weeks into February 1836, Texans and *tejanos* worked sporadically at repairing the Alamo compound—the long barracks and officers' quarters, enlisted men's barracks, the hospital, the walls, and gun emplacements. Cós' ramp in the church center remained—the battlement and cannon were to become an important part of the Texans' defense of the Alamo against the Mexicans.

At the same time other Texans, those in the settlements along the Colorado, Brazos, Red and Trinity rivers, and east to Nacogdoches, were generally undecided as to the importance of the faraway outpost in south Texas. They were more concerned about the decisions being made in Mexico City and in Saltillo, and in Monclova where the Texas-Coahuila Congress met. Sam Houston ordered Jim Bowie to blow up the Alamo, then to haul the artillery up to the river settlements. Instead the scrappy Bowie roundly protested that he and the other volunteers would "rather die in [these] ditches than give them up to the enemy."

So the matter briefly rested. Texans and *tejanos* stayed on at the Alamo, neglected by the Texas provisional government in San Felipe which dispatched little food, clothing, ammunition, or medical supplies to the remote garrison.

Ultimately, decisive action in Mexico overcame hesitation in Texas. On February 23 Santa Anna captured San Antonio de Béxar, and almost immediately Mexican forces began firing on the Alamo fort. For twelve days and nights the surrounded garrison was under siege. Then, after an ominous quiet, just past midnight on March 6 the Mexicans attacked. In a fierce pre-dawn assault the force of some four or five thousand soldiers, as variously reported, overran and slaughtered the defenders of the Alamo.

Despite Santa Anna's victory at the Alamo, and his subsequent orders to massacre Fannin's men at Goliad on Sunday, March 27, the tide of war changed when Sam Houston and his volunteers won the decisive battle of San Jacinto on April 21. As before, the defeated Mexicans gave up the Alamo, again leaving the building burning as a fiery memorial to Texas defeats and triumph.

During the next years, innumerable visitors walked amid the broken and shattered walls of the desolate "Shrine of Texas Liberty," shaking their heads at the neglect they saw. In 1846, a decade after Texas independence when the Republic of Texas joined the Union, Santa Anna declared war on the United States, claiming that Texas was part of Mexico. American military men soon arrived at the newly established military base in San Antonio and, since the centrally located Alamo complex seemed a likely place for workshops and storage depot, army engineers set about rebuilding and converting the old *convento* for new uses.

Work also began on repairs to the long-neglected Alamo church. Engineers shored up walls and added a roof—the first in over eighty years—and proceeded to change the old façade. The original roof line, broken during the Mexican attack in 1836, was rebuilt to the familiar silhouette seen today. Two frontal, second-story windows not in the early church were added in the facelift which permanently changed the design of the ancient mission. A curved parapet was also added to the horizontal eastern façade where the gunners Dickinson, Esparza and Wolfe had manned their cannon against the Mexicans. In paintings and drawings of the battle as early as 1850, this new appearance of the Alamo inaccurately began to portray its 1836 image; and later, in movies, the 1836 battle appears to have been fought in front of an Alamo façade that did not appear until fourteen years *after* the battle.

Nor were these the last changes or threats of change. In the 1850s city planners, along with business interests, converted the open Alamo plaza into a commercial area. Office buildings eventually rose to obscure the old view of the river, making the area a nest of time-worn and new structures. Blame for the Alamo's loss of land rests on its prime location; its plaza became the center of San Antonio's busy, midtown commercial district. Over the years various proposals for the site questioned and even

Alamo Plaza ca. 1900 with the new Post Office, the elaborate Honoré Grenêt general store built on the ruins of the Alamo's convento, the Alamo church, and the adjacent saloons.

ignored the historic importance of the old buildings. Which of them should be preserved and which should be torn down? Ultimately the only buildings left standing were the Alamo church, or "Shrine," which was purchased by the state of Texas in 1883 and placed in care of the City of San Antonio, and remnants of the once two-story Long Barracks, over which a warehouse and general merchandise store had been constructed.

Adina DeZavala, Texas history activist and preservationist, tried unsuccessfully after 1892 to interest Texans in securing the three acres around the Shrine. When the property came on the market at prime commercial value, she turned to young heiress Clara Driscoll. With characteristic aplomb, Miss Driscoll wrote a check for a thirty-day option, continued to provide money of her own, and ultimately contributed the major funding for purchasing the site, thus permanently adding the three acres to the Alamo grounds and providing a protective space around the Alamo church. The Daughters of the Republic of Texas, a historical organization of women concerned for the preservation of Texas history, was

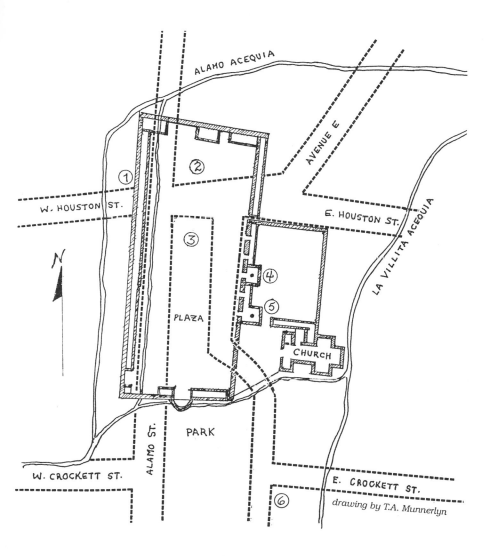

1. Gibbs Building
2. Post Office
3. Cenotaph
4. The long barrack
5. Convent
6. Menger Hotel

Map of the 1836 Alamo Complex, with an overlay of today's streets and buildings.

Cabinet photograph of the Alamo ca. 1900 during a rare snowfall, showing one of the Alamo plaza saloons. Courtesy Daughters of the Republic of Texas Library at the Alamo.

The Alamo in 1912-1913. Removal of the Grenét mercantile building revealed the ruins of the convento, but after long debate the second story walls were removed during reconstruction. Courtesy Daughters of the Republic of Texas Library at the Alamo.

designated by the state to be custodian of the Alamo property.   Miss Driscoll was later reimbursed by the Texas Legislature for the amount of her investment.

In the 1930s a museum and souvenir shop was constructed on the Alamo grounds, and in the 1950s a library and archives was added.   Offices and a maintenance building were built to support the administration and preservation of the complex.   In the 1980s new exhibits in the Long Barracks replaced earlier ones first opened to the public in 1968.   Modern stone walls now enclose the entire complex of church and buildings, set amid the grounds of lawns and plantings.

In 1836 the Alamo's walled-in plazas and buildings had clustered within an irregular rectangle of flowing *acequias.* Its large, public plaza extended north across present-day East Houston Street and about one fourth of the way onto the site of the post office building. To the west the plaza boundary extended across today's Alamo Street to the modern Gibbs building. On the east the *Acequia Madre* ran close to the rear of the church before it flowed south. What is now East Crockett Street is marginally outside the plaza's original southern boundary. From the northwest corner the wall followed the *Acequia del Alamo* to the southwest corner. The Alamo and its grounds looked westward over the San Antonio River and beyond to *La Plaza de las Islas* and *La Plaza de Armas*—today's Main Plaza and Military Plaza.

Today the complex of buildings is a lively center peopled with tourists, historians and businessmen all bound, within the framework of historic preservation and commerce, to the invisible Alamo mystique. From where Mexican forces once gathered for Santa Anna's attack, hotels now overlook the Alamo grounds, and visitors photograph the Alamo, with its 1850 façade, and Coppini's nearby monument to the Alamo heroes.

What is, perhaps, most remarkable in the Alamo's long history of defense against both military and commercial attacks, is that any of it survived at all to stand in its twentieth-century setting—an ancient jewel in liberty's enduring crown.

THE SIEGE AND STORMING OF THE ALAMO

ॐ

For wccks during January and February 1836 rumors flooded Béxar from the Río Grande—Mexican forces were gathering to invade Texas. Despite these warnings Texan and *tejano* soldiers in San Antonio did not hasten their preparations to defend against Santa Anna's army. The men stationed at the Alamo were augmented by other volunteer soldiers stationed around Main and Military plazas, but few among the Texan and *tejano* defenders had any military training, and they found but little military organization after they arrived in Béxar. Most of the American volunteers had been there only a short time, living in various places around town, eating wherever they could and sleeping anywhere they found lodgings. The foreign atmosphere at Béxar and the easy lives of the *bejareños* offered the new arrivals entertainment and charming distractions—cockfights and card games during the day and evening dances at the chaperoned *fandangos*—diverting their attention from the serious business of soldiering.

Few of the men, the volunteers or even the men in command, were uneasy over the threat of Mexican invasion so soon after December's victory over General Martín Perfecto de Cós. Surely, they rationalized, Santa Anna would not attempt to invade Texas during the winter months. No army with its horses, mules, and oxen could cross the burned out, dry, grassless prairies that lay between the Rio Grande and Béxar.

The prevailing feeling of security not withstanding, in

mid-January the Béxar commander, James Neill, wrote Texas headquarters asking for immediate aid. "I hope we will be reinforced in eight days, or we will be over-run by the enemy, but if I have only 100 men, I will fight 1000 as long as I can and then not surrender."

Neill soon left his command because of illness in his family, but work continued at the Alamo on repairing the buildings Cós had wrecked before his retreat. Weaknesses in the mission-turned-fortress would make its defense difficult, but the men patched the buildings' broken walls, closed wide gaps in the outer stockade, and pulled the cannon onto high platforms. They neglected, however, to collect adequate food stocks of dried corn and cattle for meat, and in the end the work of preparation was woefully incomplete.

As early February passed, the Texans continued to discredit the rumors of invasion. For some days a puzzled Lieutenant Colonel William Barret Travis watched *bejareños* leaving town, their carts piled high with household possessions. When he asked where they were going, the answer was always the same, "We are going to our farms." Travis was unable to stop them even though few of them were farm laborers or owned farms.

Finally *tejano* Captain Juan Seguín sent his kinsman Blas Herrera down to Mexico for an accurate report. On February 20 he returned with electrifying news—the Mexican army had crossed the Rio Grande and was already nearing Béxar! Soon afterwards, on the evening of February 22, a *bejareño* on horseback galloped into town—Santa Anna and his troops were encamped on the Río Medina, twenty-five miles southwest of Béxar. Bowie and Travis, commanders of the Alamo garrison, dismissed the fateful news as unreliable and continued their evening's entertainment at a *fandango*.

Santa Anna's cruelties were too well-known for the remaining *bejareños* to trust their fate to chance. The next morning, in the gray, early light they flung their possessions into carts and in a frenzy urged on their oxen and donkeys. People and animals jostled against each other hurrying east, out of town and into the countryside.

Only a few stayed behind, with no way to travel or unable to make up their minds to escape.

As early daylight revealed the flat, brushy landscape, a Texan lookout on San Fernando's bell tower sighted sunlight glistening on armor among the trees west of town. Two scouts rode out, only to encounter Mexican cavalry on the outskirts of Béxar. By afternoon Mexican soldiers were overrunning the town as the Alamo men raced to the fort, frantic civilians following at their heels. Among them were the women with their children who would share the coming days of terror with the fighting men.

By late afternoon the Mexicans commanded the deserted town. Officers on horseback urged their sandal-shod companies through the narrow streets. Military Plaza and the adjoining Main Plaza resounded with rumbling artillery carts, the sharp hooves of the cavalry horses, and the soft pad of foot soldiers.

Last came the Mexican women, the *soldaderas*, following with their children. They were the army's laundresses and cooks, wives and sweethearts. Settling like restless, migrating birds at the edges of the army bivouac, they dumped their bundles, shifted the *rebozos* cradling their babies, and began searching for mesquite branches and water. Fitful cookfires marked their encampment, flickering and burning with but little heat against the cold February winds. Alone on its rise above the San Antonio River crouched the walled-in Alamo.

The men who had toiled to strengthen the Alamo defenses during the weeks of January and February now barricaded the doors and remaining openings as best they could. At Main Plaza the Mexicans ran up the blood-red flag of "no quarter"—no mercy and no surrender. It flapped from the belfry of San Fernando, whipping out its message to the slender force in the Alamo. Texans and *tejanos* within the fort were now at Santa Anna's mercy.

More descriptions have been recorded on the siege and storming of the Alamo than there were men inside the mission-fortress, and more words have been written than there were bullets fired that final morning. For twelve days and nights the men of the Alamo slept but little, cradling their long rifles. Alamo gunners fired back replies to the Mexican cannon bombardment, watching as the thousands of Mexican soldiers tightened the circle around them. The Mexicans were easy to see. Months earlier Cós had cleared the land of everything blocking the view west to the plazas, cutting down the mesquites, the pomegranates and the figs, the old cottonwoods, willows and pecan trees that grew along the *acequias*.

Twice the defenders raised their voices in an exuberance of welcoming shouts—first for the thirty-two Gonzales men from the east prairie who ran into the Alamo walls on the morning of March 1, and then again for James Butler Bonham who braved the Mexican lines and galloped alone into the fortress. No additional help was ever to arrive. Both sides knew the Texas cause was hopeless; Travis drew his immortal line in the Alamo dust and Santa Anna rode among his troops coordinating his military action against the rebels.

Despite the desperate situation the women in the Alamo soon set up routines for their families. Each day the meals were the same—freshly killed beef from the cattle herd in the Alamo's corral. At first there was no coffee to help their men stay awake. For tortillas they pounded meal from corn brought in by the Alamo men who dashed outside to the deserted houses for more supplies. Later they used the corn meal and drank the coffee which the Gonzales men brought with them when they scrambled through the Alamo gates.

The women within the church, and the Navarro sisters and blacks in the officers' quarters, spent their days in much the same way, bending over small cooking fires within the protecting walls. Getting water was dangerous. Once a branch of the *Acequia Madre del Álamo* had flowed inside the plaza, but now it was cut off by the Mexicans. The recently dug well, near the church, lay in the open within range of enemy sharpshooters.

During the first days of March an Alamo gun sounded its message daily to Texas spies riding the prairie to the

1837 watercolor of the Alamo by Mary Adams Maverick. The colors of the 6-1/4" x 9-1/2" painting on rag paper are now sepia and a faded blue-green. The original is still owned by the Maverick family. Courtesy The Alamo Curator.

east—Travis' notice to the Gonzales settlement that the garrison still held. At each explosion the frightened and bellowing cattle crowded into the corners of their corral. In the center pen horses nickered and whinnied as they raced around in circles, their eyes showing white with panic.

On March 6 Santa Anna was ready to finish off the traitorous rebels who defied him in the Alamo. In the sharp cold, at the darkest morning hour before sunrise, he gave the orders to attack. "The stars were yet in the sky, and all was so still that they thrilled the air like something unearthly," novelist Amelia Barr wrote years later of the scene. The volunteers in the Alamo played out their parts in one final short violent drama, the "bloodiest, smokiest, grimmest tragedy of the century," exclaimed poet Sidney Lanier.

The battle lasted only a half-hour. In dawn's ashy light cannon blasts roared, and black smoke with the acrid smell of gun powder swirled over the open plaza and within the enclosed spaces. Rifle gunfire pierced the smoke. The women in their hiding places closed their eyes and bent over their children as the horrid chorus swelled closer and closer with shrieks, yells and curses— some stopping in mid-word.

One by one the cannons and rifles fell silent. The black smoke absorbed the echoes of battle, leaving only reverberations in the ears of the living. The dead lay still, enshrouded by lingering wisps of smoke. By nine o'clock the slanted rays of the morning sun outlined the broken lines of the church above a hushed battleground.

Victorious, Santa Anna walked with his lieutenants among the Alamo dead until the bodies of Colonels Travis, Bowie and Crockett were pointed out to him. He "ordered wood to be brought to burn the bodies of the Texans," and directed a company of dragoons to search the countryside. At about three o'clock in the afternoon of the next day, they began to build a pile of wood and dry branches, upon which some of the bodies were placed, then more wood and more bodies until all were arranged in layers. "Kindling wood was distributed through the pile, and at 5 o'clock it was lighted."

Through the night, firelight reflected on the broken Alamo façade and cast a faint glow over the artillery-pocked buildings of Main Plaza. By dawn, buzzards circled in the sky as the ashes of brave men blew across the deserted plaza.

JUANA NAVARRO PÉREZ ALSBURY

Adventurous *Tejana*

༺♠

María Juana was the eldest child of José Ángel Navarro, who chose his sister Josefa and her husband Juan Martín Veramendi as godparents on her christening day, December 28, 1812. The later christenings of Ángel's two younger daughters were not to compare with Juana's sumptuous celebration and prestigious sponsors. When their mother, Concepción Cervantes, was unable to care for the children, Juana became part of *tía* Josefa's family. Gertrudis, the second daughter, became part of Ángel's brother Luciano's household and family, and the third daughter Josefa, "Chipita," lived for a time with Luz Escalera. Yet all three girls were inheritors of the Navarro name.

Ángel Navarro, with his father (who had come from Corsica in the 1770s) and brothers, had long been important in the public affairs of Béxar. In the decade before 1821 the outspoken Navarro men and their kinsmen had chosen a dangerous stance in Mexico's rebellion against Spanish rule. Ángel and his younger brother José Antonio joined the active revolutionaries but soon were forced to flee the province of Texas for their lives. Ángel fled south below the Rio Grande; eighteen-year-old José Antonio, with his brother-in-law Juan Martín Veramendi, joined other *bejareños* to find safety in Louisiana. Thus they escaped the murderous punishment meted

The Veramendi Palace. All that remains of the luxuriously furnished home of Juan Martin and Josefa Veramendi is the wooden main door now displayed in the Alamo chapel. Courtesy Daughters of the Republic of Texas Library at the Alamo.

Rear view of the Veramendi Palace ca. 1850. Drawing by Morgan Wolfe Merrick showing the wide expanse of land behind the Palace, already showing signs of neglect, toward the river. Courtesy Daughters of the Republic of Texas Library at the Alamo.

out after 1811 by the Spanish royalists to the revolutionaries who remained in Béxar.

By 1821 Spain had lost the battle for Mexico, and Béxar became an outpost stronghold of Mexican Texas. Both Ángel and José Antonio took part in the new Mexican government, and for a time both strong-willed brothers held the same political views. After 1823, however, José Antonio, a steadfast *tejano,* grew closer to empresario Stephen F. Austin's and the Anglo-American colonists' ideas for a self-governing state. Ángel turned to Mexican dictator Santa Anna and his Centralist policies.

Juana and her cousin Ursula grew up as sisters in the Veramendi Palace, Juan Martín's headquarters as governor of Coahuila and Texas. In the late 1820s important visitors rode up to the palace just off Main Plaza—men with plans for changing a Texas left desolate in the years after Mexican independence.

The fateful decade of the 1830s began with sorrow for the Navarro sisters when their mother Concepción died. Yet their sadness was somewhat dispelled by the two family wedding celebrations the following year. First, their forty-five-year-old father, now holding the important post of *Alcalde* of Béxar, took himself a wife.

Then to no one's surprise, but to some of the family's chagrin, another marriage took place. When adventurer James Bowie arrived at the palace to discuss business with Governor Veramendi, it wasn't long before he had an additional reason for spending time in Béxar. He had fallen in love with Juan Martín's oldest daughter Ursula. Bowie "was a tall, well-made gentleman," remembered Juana, "of very serious countenance, of few words, always to the point, and a warm friend." Family and friends gathered at San Fernando Church in 1831 when Don Martín acquired a son-in-law as well as a business partner. Recalling the bright days of Bowie and Ursula's marriage, Juana shared the glow of his affections for his new family. "He was kind and so acted as to secure the love and confidence of all," she confided.

Even though Ursula's marriage to an Anglo American

may not have pleased her Centralist *tío* Ángel, yet another family wedding brought him a son-in-law he thought worthy of the Navarro name and heritage. His eldest daughter Juana married Ramigio Alejo Pérez, a young man with ties to the prominent de León family of Victoria. Juana's younger sister Gertrudis now had the pleasure and comfort of Juana's home to share when she chose.

During the summer of 1833, when Jim Bowie rode off to check on his commercial holdings in Louisiana, Ursula with their two young children joined her parents and her younger sisters and brothers in Monclova for a vacation. During early autumn, cholera swept through the Veramendi household—Juan Martín and his wife Josefa died, and soon Ursula and the two little Bowie children fell ill and perished as well.

How different Veramendi Palace became that autumn. Luciano Navarro, guardian of his sister Josefa's large family of children, moved his merchandise stock and sold it from the public rooms of the palace. Gertrudis visited there with her young cousins. During cold days the family dogs huddled near the doors, and leaves fell in yellow showers over the swept earthen patios. Lonely Jim Bowie, with several of his black servants, continued to make the palace his home. Americans and Mexicans on business called at the palace, only now they conferred with Bowie and not with Don Martín Veramendi.

The next year Juana's husband Alejo died when the cholera swept into Texas. Some records list a child Encarnación who also died, but their son Alejo, born in 1835, survived.

Ángel took these family losses to heart but also had other pressing matters needing his attention. As *alcalde* he could no longer ignore the growing American presence in Béxar nor the insistent demands from Mexico City. For as long as he could, he resisted orders to give up his municipal offices to be used as headquarters for General Cós, who was being assigned to take over the military command of Béxar. The building was well situated with access to both Military and Main plazas. Twice Ángel wrote his refusals, then cagily suggested Stephen F.

Austin's long-time friend, *tejano* Erasmo Seguín, for the honor of housing the official. Finally, having no choice, he took the Béxar archives and moved out in anticipation of Cós' arrival.

During the summer of 1835 a visitor rode into Béxar who would greatly influence Ángel's life. Dr. Horatio Alexander Alsbury, an early Texas colonist, had returned from Mexico in haste, bringing a warning to Texans and *tejanos*. Santa Anna planned to "burn houses and drive from the country a number of its principal citizens." Alsbury most likely appeared at Veramendi Palace looking for Jim Bowie, and there met the widowed Juana. After a hurried mission to the settlements on the Brazos he returned to Béxar and joined the growing number of volunteers gathered to contest Mexican control of the important town.

The political and military controls of Béxar converged in October 1835 when Cós arrived with his army and established firm control for the Mexican government. By November Mexican soldiers were skirmishing against the united forces of the Texans and the companies of local *tejanos*.

On December 5 Ben Milam launched the siege and storming of Béxar, and Texans and *tejanos* entered town from their headquarters to the north. Milam first occupied the Garza house as his command headquarters, then Colonel Johnson took over Veramendi Palace. Although several women of the household were in the palace when it was captured, Juana with her baby and Gertrudis must have fled earlier to the safety of a remote ranch. Cós, after four days and nights of violent fighting, was overwhelmed and forced to send a surrender offer on December 9. After negotiations he signed the final agreement on December 10, and within days the Mexicans retreated to the Rio Grande.

Veramendi Palace stood scarred and devastated in the battle's wake; within the rooms where Luciano Navarro kept his merchandise, the barrels, bales, and boxes of store goods lay scattered and spoiled. The usually gentle José Antonio returned to Béxar to view his losses with anger; his home and office between the plazas had been broken into; gold bullion, buried under the floors, had been found and stolen; his precious collection of books and maps and irreplaceable land records had been destroyed.

Although the Texans and *tejanos* had defeated the Mexicans, Ángel still held the office of political chief of Béxar, his allegiance to Mexico unchanged and unchallenged. At the same time José Antonio and their uncle José Francisco Ruíz remained true to their *tejano* commitment, awaiting the next move in the confrontation. Ángel, also waiting out a situation which he viewed as temporary, learned to tolerate Bowie's friend Horatio Alsbury's courting visits to Juana.

After the Mexican surrender most of the Texan volunteers at Béxar rode east to join their families, oversee the gathering of the neglected corn crops, and look over their cattle. Alsbury remained in Béxar, and in early January Juana married her suitor. In the days that followed she often watched her husband saddle his best horse to ride out with the Texan and *tejano* spy companies.

Other *bejareños* realistically faced the possibilities of a return of the Mexican forces, and prudently planned to evacuate their families to safer havens. Erastus "Deaf" Smith's resourceful wife Guadalupe Ruíz Duran, gathering her children, set off in a cart using a borrowed ox. Following the century-old Atascosito Road east to the Brazos, she fell in with other settlers fleeing the Mexicans early in the first "Runaway Scrape." John W. Smith sent his young wife, María de Jesús Curbelo, possibly with small children, on a journey all the way to New Orleans to wait out the threatening turmoil.

While *tejano* Juan Seguín joined the Alamo forces, his father Erasmo escorted the family members to East Texas to escape the threat of capture by the Mexican army. Other families continued to leave the threatened town. Juana, uncertain of what she should do, waited for her husband to decide what measures to take. Time ran out, and on February 23 Mexican armies entered Béxar.

Juana never said who escorted her, little Alejo, and Gertrudis to the Alamo. Most likely Bowie sent for them and his black servants from Veramendi Palace. Once within the Alamo walls, however, they and the servants settled near Travis and Bowie in the officers' quarters in the northwest corner of the plaza. Here they remained until the last. Where was her husband?

Diarist Mary Maverick, who interviewed Juana and her husband two years after the battle, quoted Alsbury as saying he was sent out from the Alamo "by express" for reinforcements. She also wrote that Juana "went into the Fort with Bowie to care for his comfort, he being in feeble health and having had to resign his command to Col. Travis." Juana remembered that, "Col. Bowie was very sick of typhoid fever and thought it prudent to be removed from the building" where she and his black servants were staying. A couple of soldiers carried Bowie away but he comforted the anxious Juana, saying gently, " *Hermana*, do not be afraid. I leave you with Col. Travis, Col. Crockett, and other friends. They are gentlemen and will treat you kindly." During the remaining days before the final assault, Bowie, despite his desperate illness, had himself carried back two or three times to visit with Juana and his black people. Their last meeting was several days before the fall of the Alamo. "I never saw him again, either dead or alive," she lamented.

Located in the officers' barracks, and removed from the other women, Juana looked after Alejo and, according to Pérez family lore, put him in a long dress hoping the Mexican soldiers would think he was a girl and not harm him. She considered advice that it would be best if she concealed her American name. As Dr. Alsbury's wife she would be identified with a man who had fought against Santa Anna's Centralist forces during the December siege of Béxar.

News on the first of March forced Juana to give up hope that her husband could rescue them. Word came with the Gonzales men who arrived at the Alamo command that Alsbury had accompanied them part of the way on that early Monday morning, but when the thirty-two volunteers arrived in the fort Alsbury was not among them.

When Santa Anna launched his final attack, Juana's rooms within the northwest walls were immediately entrapped as the Mexican soldiers swirled into the plaza. Her terror-filled day began at dawn as she "peeped out and saw the surging columns of Santa Anna assaulting the Alamo on every side." At the same time noises of the conflict—the thundering of artillery, the desperate voices of soldiers in conflict—welled up around her quarters.

As gunfire erupted outside their hiding place, Juana "realized the fact that the brave Texians had been overwhelmed by the numbers" of the enemy. She sent Gertrudis to ask the Mexicans not to fire into their room where there were only women, but at the door Gertrudis was met with soldiers' offensive language as they rushed in. One man grabbed her shawl, tearing it from her shoulders as she ran back toward Juana, who stood clutching her child, fearing for their lives.

A soldier followed Gertrudis in close pursuit yelling, "Your money or your husband," to which she gasped, "I have neither money nor husband!" Other soldiers, spying Juana's trunk, broke it open and grabbed up gold coins, clothes, and pieces of her jewelry. Most valuable of all were the watches Colonel Travis and other officers had given Juana for safekeeping.

In a desperate act of protecting her, a sick Texan soldier pushed aside the Mexicans and ran up to Juana, but he was bayoneted at her side. His name, she thought, was Mitchell. As the soldier fell at her feet, a young *tejano*, pursued by the Mexicans, seized her by the arm and swung her around to shield himself. Mexican bayonets plunged into him and he dropped away from her; the frenzied soldiers then fired repeatedly into his lifeless body.

A Mexican officer followed the soldiers into the room. Surprised at seeing Juana and Gertrudis, he yelled, "How did you come here? What are you doing here?" Then excitedly, "Where is the entrance to the fort?" Pushing the two women ahead of him out of their room, he left them beside a cannon. "Stand here," he ordered. "You will be sent to the President Santa Anna!"

As he dashed away another Mexican officer ran up. Seeing the two in such peril, he yelled, "Why are you women here?"

Juana shouted, "An officer ordered us to remain here—he would have us sent to the president."

"President, the devil," he yelled. "Don't you see they're about to fire this cannon? Leave here!"

Juana, clutching Alejo, grabbed at Gertrudis. Together they stumbled over bodies as they returned to their room. Unaccounted time passed in which the battle noises began to subside. Then Juana heard a voice she knew.

"*Hermana,* don't you recognize your own brother-in-law?"

The Mexican soldier who approached them was Manuel Pérez, her first husband's brother, who had gotten permission to search for them.

"I am so excited and distressed," Juana gasped, "I scarcely know anything."

Pérez led Juana and Gertrudis to the Alamo entrance, where a black woman of Bowie's household agreed to go with them to their father's home. Juana remembered hearing sporadic gunfire from the Alamo until twelve o'clock that day. One source says that sometime during the day one of the Navarros, Ángel or Luciano, sent a messenger to Juan Seguín, waiting in Gonzales for news from the Alamo after Travis had sent him out from the beleaguered fortress with a letter to Colonel Fannin asking for aid.

On the day following the battle the Alamo women had their turns at being interviewed by Santa Anna, who had offered to pardon the *tejanos* in exchange for their loyalty. In his headquarters on Main Plaza he spent little time with the distracted, disheveled women. A question or two: "Why were you in the Alamo? Do you know any *tejano* or Texan who escaped?" Juana and Gertrudis, daughters of a Mexican loyalist, drew only the dictator's disdain rather than his full wrath.

The Mexican armies soon moved out of Béxar in pursuit of Houston's fleeing command, and for several weeks *bejareños* had no information of the fate of the Texas forces. In late April, Ángel brought home a guest, Dr. Joseph Barnard, dispatched by the Mexican command at Goliad to care for the Mexicans wounded at the Alamo, who told the Navarros the horrifying news of the massacre of Fannin's men at Goliad.

Juana's wait for her husband ended when he rode into town in mid-May. She had not seen him for almost three months. He carried with him the first reliable news concerning the Texas victory at San Jacinto, and for a time he was the only source for an account of the battle. Soon Alsbury again set out on horseback, this time in the company of the women of his household—Juana, with little Alejo, and Gertrudis. Together they rode east to a Navarro ranch on Calaveras Creek.

While she was away Juana missed seeing her father, in the last stages of a desperate illness, perform a probably delirious "dance for joy" in the streets of Béxar as his erstwhile Mexican allies withdrew from town. Nor did she see the Alamo again set afire by the retreating enemy.

If Ángel often seemed indifferent to his *tejana* daughters, he remembered them in his will. His widow and four surviving children each inherited one fifth of his ranch property, and Juana and Gertrudis' share of the cattle from Ángel's once-large herds amounted to twenty-five head each. Alsbury saw to it that his young sister-in-law's *Box 4* brand marked her cattle. Each of the two sisters also received three hundred *pesos* and, since Gertrudis could not write, Juana signed the receipt for her.

After her Alamo experience Juana Navarro Alsbury signed a number of documents pertaining to her losses during the battle.

It did not take long, after the Mexicans gave up Béxar, for a tide of Americans, new to Texas, to inundate the town. Most of these new arrivals had taken no part in the independence struggle against Mexico. Some were quarrelsome, dishonest men seeking land—most often from unsuspecting *bejareños.*

The familiar pattern of life disappeared from the old town, replaced by new ways often misunderstood by the citizens of Béxar. The Navarros were among the families for whom the changes brought tragedy. Ángel's youngest brother, Eugenio, who lived in the Navarro block on Main Plaza, was murdered in the family merchandise store in 1838.

The incident involved one of the newly arrived renegades known locally as "sports," an ill-tempered gambler named Tinsley who shot the innocent Eugenio in cold blood. Although dying, Eugenio managed to stab and kill his murderer with a Bowie knife. As the Navarros gathered in sorrow, Eugenio was buried beneath the floors of San Fernando.

Nor was that the end of violence. The Texas Republic faced a long contest with Indians on the western frontier lands, and in the now-famous Council House Fight in Béxar, an arranged meeting between the Comanches and Texans in March 1840, a melee of arrows and gun shots suddenly erupted. Killed in the exchange was Brazos visitor George Washington Cayce.

Mary Maverick later described Cayce as a "very pleasant and handsome young man" who reportedly had come to marry Gertrudis Navarro, although when the engagement was made and who arranged it is unknown. Perhaps Dr. Alsbury, who was also from the Brazos, thought to make a match between a Navarro heiress and the son of one of his friends.

After Cayce's death Gertrudis may have been in mourning, for not until the following year did she marry Miguel Cantu. Possibly, during the days Gertrudis was in the Alamo, she had visited with *tejana* Concepción Charlí and come to know of *ranchero* Miguel Cantu, Concepción's grandson.

Gertrudis married Miguel and lived the remainder of her long life on the old Cantu Calavaras ranch near present day Elmendorf. They reared a large family. When she died in 1895 at the age of seventy-nine, she shared with her illustrious Navarro family well over a century of tempestuous Texas history.

Death announcement of Juana Navarro Pérez Alsbury, written by her son Alejo Pérez:

Juana Navarro y Alsbury,
The 23rd day of July of 1888,
died at 4:30 in the afternoon
at the age of 78 years
at the Rancho de la Laguna Redonda
where she is buried.
Alejo E. Pérez

Courtesy of George Pérez of San Antonio, a descendent of Juana Navarro Pérez Alsbury.

Juana, during the fifty years following her Alamo experience, continued a life of adventure. In early September 1842 she set out for Mexico to join her husband after he and fifty-two men, gathered in Béxar for a session of district court, were captured by Mexican General Adrian Woll. She traveled after the prisoners on the first leg of their march to Perote prison in Mexico, but stopped in Candela where she waited almost two years until his return.

When the United States began to recruit forces for the Mexican War in 1846, Alsbury once again joined a company of fighting men. In an 1857 testimony Juana identified herself as a widow; her husband had "accompanied the American army across the Rio Grande during the war between the United States and Mexico and in the year 1846 had been killed by the Mexicans somewhere between Carmargo and Saltillo."

Juana Navarro Pérez Alsbury died at 4:30 in the afternoon, July 23, 1888, at *El Rancho de la Laguna* near San Antonio. In her last years it was easy to understand why her morning chocolate might grow cold and her evening coffee remained untouched while her memories recalled her tempestuous life and the Texans and *tejanos* she had known—heroes of a Texas that would "never see their like again."

MADAME CANDELARIA

Heroine of Legend

ઋ

Madame Candelaria—Andrea Castañon de Villanueva—lived to become a vibrant legend with her enduring accounts of the Alamo and its heroic days of siege and defeat by the Mexican armies. Throughout her long life she steadfastly claimed to have witnessed that final battle on the morning of March 6, 1836, telling and retelling her version of the events and the actions of the men she knew there. In time, Andrea's version of the battle-turned-nightmare became legendary. "When horror is intensified by mystery, the sure product is romance," wrote Texan Frank W. Johnson of the Alamo story.

"My maiden name was Andrea Castañon," she began her reminiscences. "I was born on Saint Andrews Day on November 30, 1785, at Laredo. I am one hundred years old and three months," she told a visitor in 1885.

"I was the daughter of Spanish soldier Antonio Castañon, who had seen service in Cuba before he came to fight against the Indians at the remote presidio. My mother, Francisca Ramírez, was Mexican." At other times she said her birthplace was at San Juan Bautista, her father's station below present-day Eagle Pass.

Wherever her birthplace, Andrea said she arrived in Béxar as a young servant girl and lived in the household of flamboyant *"La Brigaviella,"* Gertrudis Pérez Cordero, wife of the Spanish governor of Texas and Coahuila. "I was in sole charge of the chocolate making for my

*Portrait of Madame Candelaria. Oil on canvas, 1891, 24" x 19-1/2",
by William Henry Huddle, a Texas painter who interviewed and
painted Madame Candelaria while studying the history of the Texas
Revolution in preparation for his paintings "Surrender of Santa
Anna" and "David Crockett." Courtesy the Hoblitzelle Collection,
Dallas Museum of Art.*

mistress," she recalled.

Soon after her arrival in Béxar she married Silberio Flores y Abrigo, a revolutionary with Father Hidalgo's Mexican uprising against Spain. He died in 1813 during the battle with Spanish Royalists on the Medina River near Béxar. Was it from that early loss that Andrea's dark eyes expressed the "sadness and tragedies of her life?"

The victorious Spaniards, leaving the dead patriots scattered on the Medina battlefield, set out to punish their kinsmen of Béxar in "a scene of barbarity" such as the *bejareños* had never before known. The Royalists first arrested a number of the local men and imprisoned them in an airless granary where many died during the fierce heat of that August summer. The Spanish commander then turned his vengeance on the women of Béxar, including Andrea. Herded into *La Quinta*, a country villa just east of the present court house, the terrified *bejareñas* were forced to kneel for hours at *metates* grinding corn and making *tortillas* for the Spanish soldiers.

The following spring the Spaniards returned to Mexico, leaving the *bejareños* to rebuild their lives and patch up their wrecked settlement. But adverse fate was not yet through with the villagers—a drought in 1819 left the land and fields around Béxar brown and desolated. Cattle and horses roamed away from their pastures bare of weeds and brush, searching for better grazing and water. *Acequias,* the network of water-filled ditches, dried up. Gardens failed—the sprouts of chiles, corn, melons, and tomatoes withered and died.

Months later, too-late and too-violent rains flooded the San Antonio River. The *acequias* spilled over their banks into the plazas and over the streets, covering everything in a layer of muddy silt and stagnant pools. Within weeks feverish diseases began to claim many of those who had survived battles, droughts, and flood. Andrea, as she was to do in later years, proved herself a skillful nurse.

The year 1821 brought peace to Béxar, at least temporarily, when Mexico became an independent nation and the years of armed conflict ceased. Except for

continuing Indian raids, life was quiet in the old settlement. Newly restored adobe houses for young families
lined the streets; repaired corrals held new horses; fresh-
cut cedar posts replaced missing ones in garden fences.
Retrenched *acequias* flowed easily and some of the deepest bog holes were filled in the dirt streets. Trade with
Mexico was reestablished, and the Military Plaza was
lined with great, two-wheeled ox carts loaded with chocolate, almonds, silk lace *mantillas* to wear to social gath-
erings, and satin slippers for dancing. Other delightful
specialties filled the Navarro and Cassiano stores and the
plaza markets.

In the 1830s Andrea married a second time. Her
husband, Candelario Villanueva, must have been a *bejareño*, for he put his mark on record in 1837 saying he
had been a resident in Texas on March 2, 1836.

For Andrea and the *bejareños* there was a season of
grace after years of turmoil. In Mexico City, however,
military leaders with their armies were fighting each
other to control the government. In Louisiana, men
looked at maps of Mexico and dreamed plans for the
thousands of uninhabited acres with no boundaries.
Mexican independence had removed the old Spanish
barriers to immigration, and eager adventurers forded
the Sabine River to cross into Texas. Following the old
Camino Real west, then south, the dusty, unshaven
Anglo Americans rode their horses into Béxar, the government center of Texas, seeking their fortunes.

During these years Andrea opened an inn, near
Alamo Plaza, where the newcomers ate and discussed the
uncertain conditions in Mexico. She listened with interest to their conversations, for "during my whole life I was
in sympathy with people struggling for freedom."

"These men," she reasoned, "are the new revolutionaries—this time against the Mexican government." *Tejanos* Erasmo Seguín and his son Juan, Placido
Benavides, and José Antonio Navarro visited with Texans
Sam Houston, Stephen F. Austin, and James Bowie as
they met at her inn while military events quickened in
Mexico. In October 1835 General Martín Perfecto de Cós

took over military command of Béxar, but against the fierce Texans and *tejanos* he had little choice but to surrender and retreat to Mexico.

While the Texans and *tejanos* worked at repairing the Alamo, Andrea became acquainted with the newly arrived volunteers who joined them. David Crockett with his moccasin-shod "Tennessee Boys" appeared in Béxar just two weeks before Santa Anna's attack, and Andrea recalled:

> They caused great excitement when they rode into Béxar. The Alamo men greeted them with heaped up bonfires to light their gathering of welcome. Crockett stood on a goods box and gave a rousing speech. I never heard such cheering and hurrahing in all my life. They stopped for supper at my hotel, and there were lots of singing, story telling, and some drinking. Crockett played the fiddle and he played it well, if I am a judge of music.
>
> He was one of the strangest men I ever saw. He was quite tall, a well-proportioned man with broad shoulders, and yet he had a face of a woman, and his manner that of a girl.

Perhaps it was the rosy complexion which appears in his portraits that seemed to her so smooth-skinned compared to the weather-beaten complexions of the *bejareños.*

Too soon the days of camaraderie ended. When Santa Anna attacked Béxar, Andrea became directly involved with the fate of the Alamo and with James Bowie in particular. In the mad scramble of last-minute fortification of the old mission Bowie fell, seriously injured while helping mount an artillery piece, then became ill with what some said was typhoid pneumonia and which others ventured was tuberculosis brought on by pneumonia. Bowie, realizing his illness was contagious, had his cot moved from the officers' quarters to the enlisted men's barracks, commonly known as the "gamblers' den," in the south wall of the plaza. Andrea's close association with Bowie began with a letter from Sam Houston. "If you wish to prove your friendship to me," he wrote her, "you will personally nurse my friend Bowie."

"Bowie was dying—dying slowly," she recalled. "He had been sick a long time, had lost considerable flesh, and now was a hulk of a man. He coughed almost incessantly, agonizingly. His pulse was rapid. He had fever. His breath was short, quick."

Despite the plea from Houston, Andrea had to think of her reputation. Going into the enlisted men's barracks, a gamblers' den, would be ruinous to the reputation of a married woman, so she changed her name to Madame Candelaria. Her married name, Villanueva, would therefore not be disgraced and she could still follow Houston's request. "Of my time in the Alamo," she said simply, "I was there five days and one night."

Through the years Madame Candelaria recounted her versions of several of the last dramas which took place inside the Alamo, among them the legend of Travis' speech offering his men only a valiant death with honor if they chose to remain within the mission-fortress. Somewhere between memory and imagination she quoted the commander's stirring message to his men:

> We must die. Three modes are presented to us. Let us choose that by which we may best serve our country. Shall we surrender and be shot without taking the life of a single enemy? Shall we try to cut our way out through Mexican ranks and be butchered before we can kill twenty of our adversaries? I am opposed to either of those methods. Let us resolve to withstand our adversaries to the last and at each advance to kill as many of them as possible. And when at last they storm our fortress let us kill them as they come; kill them as they scale our wall; kill them as they leap within; kill them as they raise their weapons and as they use them; kill them as they kill our companions, and continue to kill as long as one of us shall remain alive.

He drew his sword and marked a line in the dusty ground of the fort. It was for each man to choose—to step across the divide between life and death. All the men quickly stepped across. Bowie, on his cot, made an effort to rise but failed. With tears dimming his eyes he asked, 'Boys won't none of you help me over there?' Crockett and several others instantly sprang to his cot and carried him across. Afterwards Crockett dropped on his knees and spoke earnestly and in low tones to Bowie.

Madame Candelaria also related the story of Alamo soldier Louis Moses Rose, who would not cross the line and instead jumped over the plaza wall to save his life.

The final assault on the Alamo remained indelibly imprinted in her memory:

> I could never regard Crockett as a hero until I saw him die. He looked grand and terrible standing at the doorway of the church and swinging something bright over his head, fighting. He had fired his last shot, and had no time to reload. The cannon balls had knocked away the sand bags and the infantry was passing through the breach there. The place was full of smoke, and I could not tell whether he was using a gun or a sword. A heap of dead was piled at his feet, and the Mexicans were lunging at him with bayonets, but he would not retreat an inch. Crockett fell and the Mexicans poured into the Alamo.

As the circle of Mexican troops closed around the Alamo, Bowie's cot had been moved again, this time into the church, to a little room at the left of the main entrance. Candelaria claimed she witnessed Crockett's loading of Bowie's rifle as well as the pair of pistols which he laid at the sick man's side. She always saved her account of Bowie's death until last.

> I sat by Bowie's side and tried to keep him as

composed as possible. A dozen or more Mexicans
sprang into the room occupied by Colonel Bowie.
He emptied his pistols in their faces and killed two
of them.

I threw myself in front of him and received two
bayonets in my body. One passed through my arm
and another through the flesh of my chin.

Here, *señores,* I pull back my sleeve to show
you, here are the scars. You can see them yet. I
implored them not to murder the sick man, but
they threw me aside, out of the way. Butchered
my friend before my eyes. They thrust a bayonet
into his lifeless head and lifted him up from my
lap.

At this point Madame Candelaria would rise from her
chair to dramatize the tragic deeds of ultimate indignity,
then sit down again to finish her narrative. "I walked out
of the cell, and when I stepped onto the floor of the Alamo,
blood ran into my shoes."

After the battle Candelaria was ordered out of the
fallen fortress under guard and, with several other
women, set to work walking among the Mexican
wounded, wiping the dirt from their mouths and giving
them water. She recalled the names of three *tejanos* who
could have been in the Alamo—José or Juan Marera
Cabrera, José María Jimenes, and "a man named Jacinto
from the Texas coast." According to Juan Seguín these
three men were sent out from the Alamo as messengers
and later fought at San Jacinto. Another man whom she
recalled as "Elijio or Elias Losoya" may have been Toribio
Losoya, who did die in the Alamo.

It would be weeks before the *bejareños* received word
of the Texas victory at San Jacinto. As the Mexican army
retreated from Béxar, the newly independent republic of
Texas was left, at least for a while, to its own designs and
problems, and Madame Candelaria adjusted to a new life
in a changed San Antonio. But as the new arrivals from
the United States brought in their strengths and influ-
ences, Santa Anna was brooding over his defeats and

Madame Candelaria with her faithful dog late in the nineteenth century. She insisted the warmth of the dog, as he slept on her feet at night, warded away her rheumatism. Courtesy Daughters of the Republic of Texas Library at the Alamo.

losses. Renewing the old tactics he had used with General Cós in 1835, he again invaded Texas, sending in armed forays to harass citizens of the republic from San Antonio down to the Rio Grande.

One foray of lasting importance was Mexican General Adrian Woll's whirlwind invasion of San Antonio in early September 1842. With a thousand troops he captured the unsuspecting town and imprisoned a number of Texas men gathered there for a court session. Madame Candelaria's husband Candelario Villanueva was among them. While Woll was out of the city in an attack on a small band of Texans southeast of San Antonio at Salado Creek, Madame Candelaria contributed food for three days to the neglected captives held in the *cuarteles* on Military Plaza. Continuing her support, she handily contributed five hundred dollars to a subscription to give money to the imprisoned men. Since her husband was Mexican and held no important position in San Antonio's new government, he was released when the other prisoners were marched off to Mexico.

During the exciting decade of the 1840s the energetic Madame Candelaria sponsored *fandangos* where she caught the attention of San Antonio visitors. One writer described her as "a Mexican woman with black hair, dark even for her race, bright eyes and extraordinary activity above all with the most agile of tongues."

Throughout her long life she continued to be a resource for San Antonio's needy. To unfortunate strangers, sometimes stranded in San Antonio on their way to California's 1849 gold rush, she provided food and a little money to help them on their way west. She and her husband were the parents of four children who later watched over their mother, and through the years she cared for twenty-two orphans. On numerous occasions she provided nursing care to San Antonians who were ill and had no one to call on for help. During the smallpox epidemics in the 1860s and 1870s, she nursed the sick who were in need. Always a defender of liberty even in her old age, she put off buying a pair of shoes for herself and instead sent the money to the *Cuba Libre* movement.

Madame Candelaria and the Alamo. Artist Verner Moore White added Candelaria's image to the foreground of his 1901 painting of the Alamo, the original of which was presented to President William McKinley. Courtesy The Alamo Curator.

Despite all of her other interests and activities, Madame Candelaria continued to recount her Alamo reminiscences to a growing number of visitors, and became a living part of the growing mystique of the Alamo saga. Photographers found her a good subject for camera studies in her old age. San Antonio artist Anna H. Stanley completed a portrait of the durable heroine in 1886. William H. Huddle painted a portrait of her, and Verner Moore White included her in his painting of the Alamo in 1901, two years after her death.

Those who knew Madame Candelaria and talked to her treasured her vivid recitals of the enduring, epic story. For sixty-three years after the fall of the Alamo she maintained her impassioned vigil to the memory of the Alamo heroes.

SUSANNA DICKINSON

Anglo Woman in the Alamo

ॐ

Give me the baby—jump up behind me—and ask no questions!" The shout of Susanna Dickinson's husband reverberated through the stone walls of the Músquiz house. Santa Anna's Mexican army had captured San Antonio de Béxar, and the bells of San Fernando were ringing wildly as young Susanna grabbed up fifteen-month-old Angelina and ran out to Main Plaza. Almeron Dickinson held the baby while his wife pulled herself up behind the saddle. She grasped the baby in one arm while she put the other around his waist, holding fast as he galloped his horse up to the ford, at the "point where the Mill now is," but not in time to escape being "fired at by the incoming Mexicans."

The horse scattered spray as it splashed over the crossing then headed through *La Villita*. Nearing the Alamo Almeron reined back his horse to maneuver among the cattle being driven by a squad of Texas volunteers "into the inclosure east of the long barrack." Once free, Almeron spurred his horse to sprint through the entrance gates being swung open for them. At the same time James Bowie "with a detachment was engaged in breaking open deserted houses in the neighborhood" in search of dried corn.

Susanna did not have to be told why the sudden rush to the Alamo. After weeks of rumor, Mexican troops had been spotted near Béxar about midday and now had

Susanna Wilkinson Dickinson. Long credited with being the only woman who survived the seige of the Alamo, Susanna was, of course, the only Anglo-American woman there. In this portrait an already portly Susanna wears her hair in the style of the 1850s. Courtesy Daughters of the Republic of Texas Library at the Alamo.

quickly gained control of the town. Santa Anna had not waited until spring to reclaim Texas from the rebels.

Almeron found a place for his family inside the strong shelter of the Alamo church, and other families soon joined them. Gregorio Esparza's wife and children fled into the Alamo in early evening and settled near the ramp that led up to the gunner's platform. Here the three artillerymen, Dickinson, Esparza, and Anthony Wolfe, old friends and *compadres* from the siege of Béxar in early December, again joined in the battle against the Mexicans. It is probable that Wolfe's two young sons also shared the protected rooms with the families.

With no time to bring anything except herself and her baby, what did Susanna find to make camp with in that rough garrison? She must have been wearing the ample calico apron that all pioneer women tied over their skirts, and might have used it for Angelina's hippins or diapers. For dishes there were only the soldiers' tin cups or dried gourds, and their knives to cut the beef from the roasting sticks. As the cold February rain and wind swept through the roofless chapel, Susanna watched volunteers race outside the walls to drag in pieces of nearby huts for use as firewood.

As the days and nights of the old month passed into March, Susanna cooked for her husband and tended her baby. During the periods when the Mexicans weren't shelling the fortress she bounced Angelina on her knee to the tunes Davy Crockett played on his fiddle while the Scotsman John McGregor tried to outplay him with his bagpipes, or she carried Angelina over to visit with commanding officer William Barret Travis. On one of these visits he sat the little girl on his lap and thoughtfully threaded a woman's cat's-eye ring on a string and put it around her neck. It was for "safe-keeping," he said. The ring was his pledge from Rebecca Cummings from whom he had parted months ago on her Brazos River plantation. For Susanna, Travis' giving up the ring revealed his forebodings about never leaving the Alamo alive or seeing Rebecca again.

Although she hesitated to ask Travis about Rebecca,

she could talk to him of his young son, left in the care of
friends on the Brazos. Other men also spoke to her of
their families. Jacob Walker from Nacogdoches found
Susanna a sympathetic listener to his reminiscences of
the children he had left behind. She felt sympathy for
another Alamo man with few close ties—lonely Jim
Bowie, his young wife and little children dead, who
coughed away his life in the barracks.

Aware of the dangerous situation and needing to keep
out of the way of the Alamo men defending the plaza
walls, much of Susanna's time was spent in the half light
of their refuge beneath the cannons, with her baby and
her memories. When she was just fifteen back in western
Tennessee, the ebony-haired girl, with blue-violet eyes
the color of water hyacinths, had first won the blacksmith
Almeron Dickinson then parted from him over a foolish
lover's quarrel. Susanna had smarted at his quick engagement to another girl. When he volunteered to fetch
Susanna from her parent's cabin to go to his wedding,
their misunderstanding was forgotten and they had
eloped. In May of 1829 Susanna and her stolid new
husband twice her age had joined a party of colonists
bound for Texas.

In the Gonzales settlement Almeron, a trained crafts-
man with a knowledge of artillery and good at making
horseshoes and tools, became an important figure and a
leader among the settlers. Although Susanna could neither read nor write, she knew the important things—how
to make a home for her husband, how to take care of a
baby, how to cook, and even how to care for farm animals
when the men were away. At the same time Susanna
learned both the terror of Indian raids and mistrust for
the Mexican officials who rode over from Béxar to check
on the town's Anglo Americans. When the Mexicans tried
to take back the cannon they had given the Gonzales
settlers as protection from the Indians, the men, aware
of the importance of their sole piece of artillery, decided
to keep it. Before the Gonzales women were hurried off
to safety at the "old fort" down on the Navidad, in
anticipation of the confrontation between the two forces,

two of them quickly made a flag for the men. Using a length of unbleached homespun and black paint, they outlined a star with a cannon beneath it and bravely lettered "Come and Take It" across the bottom.

The Texans fought for their cannon and forced the Mexicans to retreat without it. As far as the men of Gonzales were concerned they had "been attacked and the war commenced!" Knowing Mexican troops in greater numbers would return, they decided to counterattack and, with Stephen F. Austin in command and their numbers swelled by newly arrived volunteers, they headed toward Béxar. Almeron joined them as artillery commander. Following a roundabout route they first swung below the town to the mission at Espada, then upriver to Concepción.

Susanna stayed behind in Gonzales during the rough and tumble weeks that followed. In November she asked Lancelot Smithers, temporarily in Gonzales, to look after her house when she fled a "mob in town." She finally heard of Almeron's success with the artillery during the victorious siege and storming of Béxar and, when he returned bringing more cannon to the Gonzales settlement, the two agreed they would return together to his new post in Béxar.

"Twined and intertwined, as dewy vines, our love will be," Susanna hummed as she gathered up clothes and dishes and pots to take along. She and baby Angelina were going to Béxar. "Going to Béxar. Going to Béxar," Susanna rhymed to the slow gait of her pony following the Gonzales Road west that winter's day.

When she sighted the tower of San Fernando on the horizon, Susanna unwound the tightly bundled baby in her arms and held her high. "See the old town," she directed, pointing the baby toward their new home. Angelina kicked her feet and waved her arms in excitement. No fears troubled Susanna—she and the baby were with Almeron. She had no foreboding that the three of them would never follow the trace together again, or that in a few weeks only she and her baby would travel this road back east to Gonzales.

In Béxar Almeron and Susanna set up housekeeping in the Ramón Músquiz building on Main Plaza. The Masonic ties between Músquiz and Dickinson created a bond of friendship between their wives, *Señora* Francisca Castañeda, the *bejareña*, and Susanna, the Texan. Yet in that small neighborhood not all acquaintances developed into friendships. While the gregarious Susanna cooked meals of cornbread and roasted beef for several volunteers of the Alamo and Béxar garrisons, the Navarro sisters on the other side of Main Plaza lived within their circle and kept to their own families and households.

Susanna's memories helped her spend the agonizing days while Almeron and the other men in the Alamo hoped for reinforcements. She constantly heard the hope voiced, "Surely, Fannin will march up that Goliad Road." With Fannin's four hundred men they could hold their own against Santa Anna. The reality of their situation was sobering—they were less than two hundred men, some ill, pitted against thousands of well-armed Mexican soldiers.

Each day brought waning hope. Susanna talked with Almeron at night, then watched him run up the ramp to his artillery post when called by the Alamo night watch. Outside noises and Spanish shouts drifted easily across the plaza as the Mexican encampments pulled nearer to the little fort. From both sides rifle fire cracked and whined while the artillery boomed and thundered.

"Nothing good could come of it all." Most of the men agreed with artilleryman Henry Warnell. If they could just get "out on the open prairie" and away from the crumbling walls of the hapless Alamo, they could fight an even battle. Crockett voiced his dissatisfaction, "I think we had better march out and die in the open air. I don't like to be hemmed up."

Susanna's spirits soared when thirty-two Gonzales volunteers rushed into the Alamo on the first day in March. All of them were men she and Almeron had known well during their own years in the settlement. Susanna, recalling their wives and their children, worried at their being left behind so defenseless in Gonzales. But surely more men would follow them, hundreds more, as soon as Fannin and his volunteers came up from Goliad. Peeping through a hole in the east wall Susanna's gaze followed Travis' messengers on horseback as they galloped off day after day carrying letters urging Texans to come to the aid of the besieged Alamo. The messages were futile—no soldiers could safely pass through the Mexican encirclement.

Susanna, balancing Angelina on her hip, leaned against the church door viewing the drama as Travis pulled out his sword and drew a line—that fateful line—in the dirt of the plaza yard. He stepped across it first, looked at his men, then asked volunteers to join him. His plea for valor moved them and soon only two men remained behind. After Bowie had his cot lifted across the line one man stood alone on the other side. She thought his name was Ross and that he did not feel he could give up his life for so hopeless a cause. At nightfall he jumped over the wall and was gone. Years later a man named Moses Louis Rose, living in Nacogdoches, testified that he had indeed escaped the Alamo.

Was Travis' brave line an answer to the fateful news James Butler Bonham had brought in his legendary gallop through the Alamo gates amidst a hail of Mexican bullets? "Expect nothing from Fannin," was Bonham's report, "He turned back to La Bahia before he was even started." Any reinforcement of the fortress was now in the hands of members of the ad interim government, squabbling at far-away Washington-on-the Brazos.

Inside the church Susanna and Almeron shared hot tea with the loyal Bonham. The little Esparza boys wrestled and played in the dusty rooms nearby. Perhaps the youngest Wolfe boy joined them while his older brother spent his time among the men. *Señora* Losoya with her two children settled their meager possessions within the church and eagerly awaited her son Toribio, when he had time away from his soldier's duties. The other women and children in the Alamo shared the hours of uncertainty but, as in Béxar during more peaceful times, although Susanna knew of the Navarro sisters she had little contact with them or Bowie's servants who remained across the plaza in the officers' quarters.

In the pre-dawn of March 6 to the bugle notes of the cruel *degüello,* Santa Anna launched his massive attack against the small force of men within the walls of the little garrison, and the women and children in the church crowded into the small southwest room for protection. As the fighting intensified Almeron found Susanna and held her a moment. "Good God, Sue, the Mexicans are inside our walls! All is lost! If they spare you, save my child!" Then, "with a parting kiss, he drew his sword and plunged into the strife." She never saw him again. Almeron Dickinson and Gregorio Esparza fell beside their cannon.

For years afterward Susanna told and retold segments of the Alamo story as she remembered it. Recalling the roster of dead heroes, like a funeral bell tolling their names, she recounted what she knew of their last minutes. "Crockett ran into my room and fell on his knees beside me. He committed himself to his God, went out and was soon killed."

She particularly remembered the Gonzales volunteers. Her most poignant memory was of eager sixteen-year-old Galba Fuqua. During the battle, he found her hideaway, perhaps hoping she could take a message home for him. "I looked at him in horror—he was holding his jaws together with his hands. Blood trickled from his mouth. He tried to speak to me, then with an agonizing gaze tried to make me understand." But Susanna could only shake her head. "The boy turned and ran out to his death."

In quick succession three unarmed Texans fled to her room, only to be shot. Jacob Walker followed, pursued by Mexican soldiers who shot him then lifted up his body on their bayonets "like a bundle of fodder."

Major Robert Evans "crawled into the room where we women were," she recalled, "not to seek refuge, but to carry out an order previously given and generally understood. If the garrison fell, the last living man was to fire the powder supply by flinging a burning brand at the

"El Deguello", the ancient call to fight to the death with no quarter, used by the Mexican Army to signal the final attack on the Alamo. Courtesy The Texas Composers Collection, The Center for American History of The University of Texas at Austin.

opening of the magazine. Evans, wounded and spent with weariness, was making his painful way across the chapel to set off the final blast only to be shot down in a Mexican crossfire."

With the defenders all dead, as Mexican soldiers roamed the smoking ruins the women, fearful for their safety, crowded with their children against the wall of their room. Suddenly a Mexican officer stopped at the doorway and called out loudly, "Is Mrs. Dickinson here?" Some say the man was the staff officer Colonel Juan Nepomuceno Almonte, for he spoke good English. One version says Susanna did not respond and he asked again. This time she dared speak. "Yes," she answered.

"If you wish to save yourself, follow me," he directed.

Susanna showed Almeron's sheepskin Masonic apron to the officer, hoping her captor was a fellow Mason and would spare her life. Whatever his reaction to the Masonic message, she was escorted away separately. Susanna missed little as she stepped slowly among "heaps of dead and dying." She recognized Crockett's mutilated body lying "between the church and the two-story barracks building, his peculiar cap by his side."

When a stray gunshot hit Susanna in the calf of her right leg, she was carried to the Músquiz house where she was treated then spent the night with the other women and children from the Alamo. The next day Santa Anna, having little time to waste, summoned the women before him.

During Susanna's interview he proposed an amazing scheme to send her and Angelina to Mexico, where the little girl would be reared as his daughter! The child would have an education and fine clothes along with all the privileges of an aristocrat. Susanna refused. Not until Colonel Almonte addressed the general in her behalf, recalling that during the time of his education in New Orleans, Americans had treated him with great kindness, did Santa Anna accept her decision.

Susanna asked to see her husband's body, but by then Almeron's body was already on a funeral pyre along with the other Alamo men. Upon her return to the

Músquiz house she recalled, "I came to my right mind—
the reality of my situation stared me in the face. I broke
down with grief and for several days my emotion was
beyond control."

Santa Anna decided that Susanna would carry his
message of the Alamo's defeat, and on March 11 she
mounted a Mexican pony, took Angelina in her arms, and
set out toward Gonzales with a Mexican escort. Ben,
Almonte's free black servant, rode along with her. At
Cibolo Creek (the Texans called it Sea Willow) the two
went on without their escort.

The next day Travis' servant Joe, when he was sure
they were not Mexicans, jumped out at them from the tall
grasses beside the road. After the battle he had been
spared but had run away toward Gonzales. They continued together, Joe walking beside them. During the last
part of the journey when three horsemen appeared far up
the road, Joe rushed to hide again in the grass, fearing
Indians or Mexican soldiers.

The horsemen, however, were from San Houston's
army at Gonzales—Henry Karnes, Erastus "Deaf" Smith,
and Robert Handy, who had set out to scout for news of
Béxar. Susanna immediately sobbed out the story of the
Alamo's fate and warned that the Mexican army was on
the march. General Sesma was at that moment headed
from Béxar to Gonzales with seven thousand soldiers.
She handed the men Santa Anna's long, handwritten
ultimatum addressed to the Texan forces—rebel soldiers
would be punished but other Texans found innocent
could assume their lives as dutiful Mexican citizens.
Henry Karnes and Robert Handy immediately galloped
back with the information, but "Deaf" Smith stayed
behind and for a time carried Angelina as they rode.

A few miles from Gonzales the exhausted survivors
stopped for the night with the Bruno family. How welcome to be in the presence of friends. Susanna bathed
Angelina and perhaps received a change of her blood-
stained clothing. By the time she reached Gonzales the
town was in an uproar of fearful and weeping women who
called out the names of their menfolk who had gone off

to the Alamo. Again and again Susanna could only answer, "Yes, he died. Yes-Yes-Yes!" Later she would wonder at her strength, not yet fully aware of her own widowhood even though she knew Almeron had already been dead almost a week.

The next evening Susanna joined what came to be known as the Runaway Scrape, ox-drawn carts filled with women and children fleeing ahead of the retreating Texas troops. When she dared look back, it was to see flames of the burning town against the night sky, a part of old Texas disappearing forever.

It is uncertain how soon Susanna settled in Houston after the battle of San Jacinto. In the late fall of 1836 she was in Columbia, applying for a widow's pension from the Texas legislature, but they did not want to set a precedent of giving away public moneys to veterans' widows so soon after the revolution. Several years later a petition to help Angelina, the "Babe of the Alamo," met with no more favorable action than had her mother's.

Susanna lived in poverty during her almost two decades of residence in Houston, despite three marriages there. In 1837 she tried to establish a home with a John Williams (a number of men of that name are listed in early Texas records). All that is known of him is found in Susanna's divorce petition in early 1838 citing his "cruelty and barbarity" to her and Angelina. In late 1838 she married Francis P. Herring, a water carrier whose death in 1843 left her widowed for a second time. In 1847 Susanna married for the fourth time, but she and Peter Bellows, a drayman, must have shared a tempestuous union. Susanna left him temporarily in 1854, then separated from him permanently and moved to Lockhart. He filed for divorce in 1857, and the proceedings were uncontested.

Angelina fared no better in her marriages than her mother. In 1851 Susanna found her daughter a satisfactory husband in John Maynard Griffith, a prosperous Montgomery County farmer. They were the parents of three children whom Angelina dutifully named Almeron, Susanna, and Joseph (for Susanna's fifth and last hus-

Angelina Dickinson. Texas granted her fame but no fortune as "The Babe of the Alamo." Courtesy Daughters of the Republic of Texas Library at the Alamo.

band). The loveless marriage in a rural setting ended in divorce and Angelina left home. From that time her life became an acceleration of tragedies, and memories of lost opportunities must have often haunted her: Santa Anna's offer of adoption and a life of education and ease; and the Texas Legislature's voting down a small pension for Almaron Dickinson's poverty-stricken young daughter.

From Montgomery County the blond, blue-eyed Angelina went to Galveston, where she met Jim Britton. No marriage license for the two has been located, although some years later Angelina was known there as "Em Britton." With the outbreak of the Civil War, Britton returned to his home in Tennessee where he joined the Confederate forces. Angelina remained behind in Galveston, but as her parting gift she gave him William Barret Travis' hammered-gold, cat's eye ring which both Susanna and Angelina had treasured.

Years before, the ring had begun its precarious journey as a gift from another woman to a man she loved who was also leaving for war—Rebecca Cummings' tender remembrance to young William Barret Travis as he rode away from the Brazos for San Antonio de Béxar and the Alamo. It would be over a century before the ring would find its way back to the Alamo; perhaps considering it a too-poignant remembrance of the Angelina he had left behind, Britton gave it to fellow Confederate DeWitt Anderson who wore it until his death in 1902. A kinsman T. H. McGregor inherited the ring; in turn his son Douglas McGregor, a Houston attorney, became the owner and presented the legendary ring to the Alamo museum in the 1950s. The ring came to rest at last at the Alamo, not far from the officers' quarters where Travis had given it to the infant Angelina and where he had fought and died that fateful sixth of March, 1836.

In the early 1860s Angelina was in New Orleans, where she married Oscar Holmes. The couple had one daughter, Sallie. How the marriage ended is uncertain, but she returned to Galveston where she led a rootless life, forming a number of liaisons before she died in the

1870s. Any marker on her grave disappeared when the waters of Galveston Bay flowed over the island during the 1900 hurricane.

Susanna reared Angelina's two younger Griffith children, Susanna and Joseph, while the elder boy Almaron grew up in his Uncle Joshua Griffith's family. Years after her death, Angelina's grandchildren joined other Texans in organizations which honored the people and places of the Texas Revolution which Susanna and Almaron had helped memorialize.

In Lockhart, soon after her divorce from Bellows, Susanna married Joseph W. Hannig, a fifth marriage which brought pleasant changes after her years of misfortunes. The couple moved from Lockhart to Austin where she was not allowed to forget her Alamo experience. Some time before the Civil War she began giving depositions for the heirs of fallen Alamo men. After the war she became something of a national celebrity, granting newspaper interviews to journalists who came to hear her story. The crowning event near the end of her life was a visit to the Alamo in 1881, forty-five years after she had limped away from the devastated ruin. Following her escorts through the various rooms within the dark church, with tears in her eyes she identified places she remembered, even the "arch overhead and the corners."

Two years later in 1883, Susanna Dickinson Hannig died in her Austin home. In 1976 a marker in the shape of Texas was placed in the state cemetery in honor of this remarkable Texas heroine.

Statue of Toribio Losoya in San Antonio. This monument to the son of Concepción Charli stands just northwest of his birthplace on Alamo Plaza. Created by Texas sculptor William Easley, the life-sized bronze was commissioned by the Coors Brewing Company and dedicated in 1986. Photo courtesy of Thomas A. Munnerlyn.

CONCEPCIÓN CHARLÍ GORTARI LOSOYA

Heroine of Revolutions

ટ&

T*ejana* Concepción Charlí Gortari Losoya survived the twelve-day siege and the final day of attack on the Alamo, although her son Toribio Losoya perished fighting alongside the other heroic Alamo defenders. How she came to be in the Alamo, and exactly when she joined the other women with their children to hide within the old church, and what instant and frantic decisions she made on that fateful February afternoon are intriguing questions which remain unanswered.

Did she run to the Alamo with her daughter Juana and younger son Juan because Toribio was already there? Or did he, knowing his mother and his brother and sister were still in town, run out from the imperiled garrison and rush them inside its strong walls? Apparently his wife María Francisca, with their little son, had already found safety elsewhere in the town.

Born in June 1779 within the shadow of the Alamo when Texas still belonged to Spain, as far back as Concepción could remember she had lived near the old mission's comfortable presence. As was the Catholic custom, within days of her birth she was christened and given the name María Concepción Norberta de los Ángeles Charlí.

Her mother María de Estrada was of Spanish parentage. Her father, Pedro de los Ángeles (Pierre des anges) Charlí was French. As a child Concepción listened to her father's stories of adventure at the Spanish Presidio Los Adaes, in East Texas, before he had been transferred to the mission San Antonio de Valero.

Her parents were important members of the Alamo mission community. María de Estrada owned cattle and acquired land of her own on the flowing *Acequia Madre* near the Alamo. Pedro Charlí worked at several jobs in the mission complex, by turns sacristan, craftsman-carpenter for the mission priests then, changing the tools of his trade, trimmer of beards and hair.

At first Concepción's parents lived in the "sixth building on the west," outside the walls that bounded the mission's public plaza. She was probably born there and grew up beside the sparkling waters of the *acequia* as it channeled south, then west to join the San Antonio River. Sometime during her girlhood the priests, in gratitude for Pedro's faithful services, granted him the carpenter shop in the southwest corner of the plaza wall. He also received, at the same corner, a stone house and land for a garden plot with water rights for irrigation from the *acequia.*

Some sources say Concepción was fifteen when she married Miguel Ignacio Gortari, a man twice her age with large ranch holdings near Béxar. They were the parents of three living children, two sons and a daughter. When her husband died around 1800 Concepción became a woman of property and also inherited her father's home and other buildings of his estate.

But the young widow did not long remain single. It was no surprise to her friends when Concepción married master tailor Bentura Losoya, whose family were Charlí neighbors. With the marriage Concepción became a bride of destiny, joining her fate with her husband's bold family and sharing first hand the rigorous years of their revolutionary experiences.

The Losoyas were volatile patriots and activists. Three generations of the men were active in the long struggle for freedom, first against Spain then against Mexico.

Concepción's father-in-law Miguel, her brother-in-law Domingo, and finally her son Toribio all took stands against oppressive governments. Her new family's devotion to liberty in Texas extended back to the mid-1770s when Miguel Losoya and a number of other Spanish subjects relocated at San Antonio de Valero from the Presidio de Adaes. Having lived near the Louisiana border, Miguel had come into contact with the exciting new ideas of the French philosophers concerning the rights of man in human society. Even in the remote twin outposts of San Antonio de Béxar and San Antonio de Valero, Miguel found others who shared his revolutionary ideas. In 1810 the fervor for independence from Spain became a revolution, and the insurrection in Mexico flared into Texas. In 1813, however, the hopes for independence were crushed, and the Spanish Royalists added Texas to their list of areas to discipline.

Cruel reprisals followed against the *bejareños*. Revolutionaries like Miguel Losoya gathered his two sons and their families, eluded the Spanish cavalry, and followed the *Camino Real* to Louisiana. Concepción and Bentura made the long journey with little Toribio and her Gortari children, Eligio, Miguel, and María de los Santos. Soon after the family arrived in Natchitoches, another daughter Juana Francisca was born.

In Béxar the Spanish authorities punished the revolutionist Miguel Losoya by confiscating and selling his property in 1819. It is not known if he lived to return to Texas with his family after Mexico's independence in 1821, but Concepción and Bentura eventually brought their family back to live in her childhood home. The Charlí house had been too close to the Alamo post to escape the gunfire and cannon blasts between the Spanish and Mexicans, and it offered poor shelter until the broken walls were reset with whole stone and adobe, and a new cover of mortar and gravel laid over the roof beams. During the peaceful years of the 1820s the Gortari children married, and *madrinas* and *padrinos* later gathered at the christenings for Concepción's grandchildren. She and Bentura were pleased when Juan, their third and last child, was born—another son to carry the Losoya name—but then Bentura died.

Afterwards she wore a black, silk lace *mantilla* in memory of her husband. On the second of each November, the Day of the Dead, Concepción and her Losoya family would gather to remember Bentura, buried in the *campo santo* west of Béxar. Kneeling beside her husband's grave, she gathered up dry stems of old flowers and set out fresh, yellow marigolds. At noon they shared small dishes of food brought for their lunch.

In the continuing balance of her family's sadnesses and joys, Toribio brought home his bride María Francisca Courbiere, a descendant of French settlers of Béxar. In yet another change Concepción's brother-in-law Domingo sold his property near the Alamo and moved to a ranch on the Medina River at Losoya Crossing southeast of Béxar.

Even as *bejareños* prayed for the blessings of peace, in the hub of far away Mexico former compatriots of the independence revolution became bitter rivals for political control of the new republic. Ultimately General Santa Anna overwhelmed his one-time comrades-at-arms and grasped the leadership of the far-flung nation, but his harsh Centralist governmental controls met with strong opposition from those who had supported a Federal system of government. In Texas the American settlers on their farms and plantations east of the Guadalupe River began talking of their own revolution—this time against Mexico—and in Béxar the *tejanos* held to their long commitment to freedom.

During the last months of 1835, when General Martín Perfecto de Cós and his army followed the Goliad Road into Béxar to reorganize the garrisons and strengthen defenses, he selected a strategic cannon site on the southwest corner of Alamo Plaza—at Concepción's house. With little notice she was forced out to make room for Cós's new fortifications. Construction began in a flurry as loads of stone and earth filled in her old home.

With hostilities imminent, Concepción had two choices. One was to join the distressed women and children who left their homes and fled up river to the Texans' and the *tejanos'* main camp where Juan Seguín and his *tejano* scouts could offer them protection. Or, instead, she could flee south along Mission Road to brother-in-law Domingo's ranch on the Medina River. Although his family would offer her welcome, he himself was no longer there. The call of freedom had again lured him off weeks earlier, and he had ridden away to join in the revolt against Mexico. Young Toribio, following his uncle's decision, soon followed other *tejanos* into the conflict of arms at Béxar.

After four days and nights of hard fighting Cós asked for peace, but Concepción's hopes of regaining her old home after the Mexican retreat were in vain. Instead, work began on repairs of the shattered Alamo, and the eighteen-pound cannon remained on the Charlí corner.

After their hard-won victory the Texas volunteer soldiers, confident Santa Anna would put off his threatened offensive against Texas until spring, took their time in repairing the battle-scarred Alamo. *Bejareños*, however, had different ideas. Why would the dictator give the rebels time to strengthen their defenses, especially when Cós reported their dogged fearlessness in battle? Knowing Santa Anna, the more knowledgeable residents feared the tactics he might use against Béxar. Would he not seek out and kill the disloyal *tejanos* as he had slaughtered resisting Zacatecas citizens only months earlier?

Many *bejareño* families, not waiting for the possible arrival of the Mexican army, fled the town in fear that Santa Anna had included their names on his list of traitors. Concepción lingered, uncertain as to what she should do, until midday on February 23 as the bells of San Fernando rang frantically and Mexican soldiers spilled into the Military and Main plazas. Too late to escape, Concepción and her children, Juana and Juan, could only run into the Alamo. No record indicates where she set up their camping place, but most likely they stayed within the few church rooms near the other women.

During the next days Concepción must have prepared food for Toribio as well as her younger children, for the volunteers had little time for cooking. All about them lay unfinished jobs—walls to shore up, trenches to dig. Night and day they took turns as lookouts watching the enemy's movements.

For twelve days and nights the siege continued until the early morning darkness of the thirteenth day. From her dark refuge Concepción could hear showers of bombs and cannon balls falling onto the Alamo compound. *Tejano* and Texan shouted to one another—directions, questions, warnings. At times she thought she recognized Toribio's voice. "That is my son," she would say to herself, making the sign of the cross over her breast, praying for the Virgin of Guadalupe's protection from the gunfire of Santa Anna's wrath.

Concepción and the other women clustered together with their crying children clinging to them, then fled to the strongest place—the small room just inside to the right of the church's main door. Louder than thunderbursts, the deep belches of artillery were punctuated by the cracks of gunfire. Smoke and dust billowed into their hiding place. For what seemed an endless time they waited, then the firing and shots stopped and an eerie quiet settled among the living and the dead. Questions filled the women's minds—who was now left to help them? Would they, too, be killed?

Not until full daylight did anyone come to their room, then an officer appeared and ordered them all outside. Following his directions they walked carefully across the plaza, threading around the dead men's bodies. Concepción, fearing she might see Toribio among them, forced herself to look at the corpses, but her son was not among the many she recognized.

Free of the Alamo walls Concepción looked up to the open sky. March winds had blown away February's clouds and she breathed in the crisp air heavy with gun powder and wood smoke. Across the river footbridge they hurried west on Potrero Street, a scraggly flock as they dodged among the exhausted soldiers roaming the battle's debris. The stunned refugees were crowded against the rows of ruined houses and banked trenches that cluttered the way. The Esparza boys held their noses as they steered clear of the ill-smelling litter left by the morning's battle. At Main Plaza their guards herded them to Ramón Músquiz's official headquarters, a familiar place to all *bejareños.* Concepción's eyes darted among the soldiers in the crowd. She saw no women.

"Toribio's wife must be safely hidden," she thought. It was good not to find her daughter-in-law in the midst of such fearful company. Years later in a petition filed for her husband's service in the Alamo, María Francisca claimed that she had been in the town and, soon after the battle, had gone with the curate into the Alamo and had identified Toribio's body as it lay among the dead.

At the Músquiz house the women drank hot coffee and fed their children from plates of food given them, their relief at being alive overshadowed by grief and their fear of Santa Anna. Concepción and the other women and children slept that night in the Músquiz building.

Early the next morning the women captives received instructions to appear before Santa Anna at the nearby Yturri house. Concepción smoothed her tangled hair and pushed the strands away from her face—the gestures gave her strength. She leaned over to Juan and brushed at the mud on his shirt. Juana rubbed dirt-stained hands over her face and up into her matted hair. When she heard the name Charlí Losoya called, Concepción clutched Juan's hand, pulled the *rebozo* about her shoulders and, with Juana beside her, stepped out into Main Plaza.

No record has been found of Santa Anna's words to Concepción. The "Napoleon of the West" had little time for disheveled women and whimpering, grimy children. With two *pesos* and a *serape* he dismissed Concepción to find her own way wherever escape lay. With the main Mexican armies moving eastward away from Béxar, south was the direction Concepción chose toward a safe haven. Domingo's ranch again offered a temporary place to wait out the situation.

(handwritten document excerpt) heirs and assigns forever.

ors, to warrant and forever defend the title to the said premises, unto the said _Jesus_

ors, ór any person claiming the same, by or through me, them, or any of them; and again

· day of _June_ in the year of our Lord o

Concepción ✝ Charlí [L.S.]
mark

Concepción Charlí's "mark". As a woman with considerable holdings, Concepción Charlí made her mark on numerous deeds of gift, land exchanges and sales. Courtesy Daughters of the Republic of Texas Library at the Alamo.

Weeks passed before *bejareños* could attempt to live once more in their houses. When Concepción finally returned to Alamo Plaza for the first sight of what had once been her home at the Charlí corner, she viewed complete destruction. Yet under the rubble the land was hers, and in time she began the rebuilding of her home. During the construction, the north wall of the house was extended over onto her kinsman Jesús Cantu's property, but the mistake was settled with an exchange of lots and a redrawing of boundaries.

Although Concepción never learned to write, she made her mark numerous times before notaries on various legal documents pertaining to her inherited lands just as, years before, her husband Miguel Gortari had signed his mark to records concerning his ranches and cattle. Tears may have clouded her eyes on the day in 1850 when she took up a pen and acknowledged a deed giving a portion of her Alamo land to her son Elijo's four children. He had been killed by Indians as he walked on the streets of Béxar. Her other Gortari son, Miguel, had also died at the hands of Indians raiding the vulnerable town.

Today, in the search for memories of Concepción Charlí, visitors need only cross the street west of the Alamo to read the marker that mentions the Alamo heroine. On this site at the southwest corner of the ancient plaza, Concepción Charlí's long-time dwelling place stood. Down a few steps and to the northwest on Losoya Street, stands a bronze statue of a fighting *tejano*, a memorial in honor of Toribio with a bandana tied over his head, an 1824 flag of a free Mexico in his left hand, and a pistol in his right.

These commemoratives, located in the shadow of the old Alamo, celebrate two of the gallant spirits of a remarkable *tejano* family—Toribio Losoya who gave his life in affirmation of his revolutionary heritage and his mother, Concepción, stalwart heroine of revolutions.

Gregorio Esparza. Texas artist Cecil Lang Casebier painted the husband of Ana Salazar de Esparza in action during the final battle. The large painting now hangs in the Alamo chapel. Courtesy The Alamo Curator.

ANA SALAZAR DE ESPARZA

Faithful *Tejana* Wife and Mother

૨૦

The Alamo experience of Ana Salazar de Esparza was described by her eldest son, Enrique, many years afterward. Widowed when her daughter, María de Jesús, was but a few days old, Ana's second husband Gregorio was a *tejano*, a soldier active in the forces gathered to fight for a democratic Texas. The Esparza family—Ana, Gregorio, eight-year-old Enrique, the two younger boys Manuel and Francisco, and Ana's eleven-year-old daughter María—lived on *Calle de Acequia*, not far from Main Plaza. Ana had come to think it was much too close. Only the past December the Mexican General Cós and his soldiers had battled *tejanos* and Texans there in the siege and storming of Béxar.

Gregorio had served as an artilleryman during the vicious battle on the plaza, and his nearby house was no place for a defenseless family as artillery bombardment and rifle fire crisscrossed the plaza in a deadly pattern. Some *tejana* women and their children fled up river to the main camp north of town to join the men of their families, and Ana and her children might have found safety there, too. Wherever she was, as the smell of gunpowder and smoke spread over the countryside, Ana prayed for Gregorio.

The course of the December battle changed when Mexican *soldaderas* and *bejareñas* loyal to Mexico, seeing a number of Mexican cavalry heading south from town in seeming retreat, collected their children and rushed up to the Alamo. Fearing Cós would surrender and leave them to the mercies of the rebels, they clamored through the gates "with cries and tears." Pushing into his quarters they found him in bed and, ignoring his protests, demanded his immediate protection.

Faced with his cavalry's desertion and overwhelmed by too many civilians and horses within the Alamo grounds, the general had no choice but to surrender. Despite their fears, the peace terms were easy on the *bejareños* loyal to Mexico, and they returned safely to their homes among the victorious Texans and *tejanos*.

Cós left his mark on the town before he marched his army back to Mexico. During the three days before he retreated he had the Alamo fortifications burned and destroyed, leaving behind a blackened shell. For weeks afterward Gregorio and his comrades spent each day at the Alamo in the slow work of repairing what Cós had ruined, but the Texans worked with little urgency, believing it would be spring before the Mexicans might return. The *tejanos* were less sanguine, and their fears were justified when, even before the new year, the Mexican dictator began the second Texas campaign. Riders brought word from the Rio Grande of troops crossing the river and on the march into Texas. Battle-wise *tejanos* and *bejareños* loaded ox carts with what they would hold, put their children on top and headed for safer havens, some fleeing eastward toward far away Louisiana.

Ana and Gregorio made arrangements with their good friend, John W. Smith, for a wagon to take the family to San Felipe, but they waited until too late. Enrique recalled that even as Mexican soldiers were marching into Béxar, Smith rushed to their house to tell Ana that no wagon could be found for them. Gregorio, hearing the news, ran down from the Alamo to see about his family. They had not gotten away, and now the only place for safety was in the Alamo with him.

Glancing quickly about the house, Ana thought of food and gathered up what she could find. The dried corn—would she find a *metate* and *mano* to grind it in the dusty rooms of the Alamo? The dried meat she wrapped in a cloth and placed beside the corn. Young María shook out the *serapes* they slept on, then grabbed up her little brothers' long shirts, rolling them all together. She pulled the family's little picture of the Virgin of Guadalupe from the wall and tied the string with the picture around her neck. Now the precious image would be safe with her, wherever the family went.

Enrique and his father led the way to the Alamo carrying some of the household goods as María pulled her little brothers along by the hand. Ana followed folding a candle and more clothes into her *rebozo* as she gave one last look at their home.

Enrique remembered that the February daylight was almost gone when they finally scampered up the hill toward the Alamo. Crossing the foot bridge on what is now Commerce Street they hurried on, wading through the *acequia* that bordered the Alamo walls. Sounds of gunfire followed them from the plazas of Béxar.

The boy recalled that the Alamo doors were "closed and barred" when the family pounded in vain to be let in. Around the side of the church Gregorio climbed through a window then leaned down to pull in the smaller boys and María before Enrique climbed in. Ana handed up her laden *rebozo*, then clasped Gregorio's strong arms to be lifted inside. All the family were now within the temporary safety of the Alamo church walls.

Gregorio settled his family beneath the

open gun emplacement high above the church. From his artillery station he could see both his family below and out toward the west to Béxar, now a Mexican army encampment. To the east, over the prairies, lay the outpost at Gonzales with its hoped-for aid. From San Antonio the Goliad Road swung southeast to the mission-fortress at La Bahia, from where Fannin and his men were expected to reinforce the Alamo volunteers.

In the darkness of their first evening in the Alamo María spread the *serapes* and Ana unwrapped the food. "A good supper will make us all sleep well," she thought. But the February night was cold within the burned-out church, and the children were restless in their drafty shelter.

Ana's days soon fell into a pattern. She sent Enrique up to Gregorio with beef which the Alamo men had roasted, and sometimes Ana and Susanna Dickinson sent food up to the other men at the artillery station. Ana waited until the safety of darkness to send María out to the well in the plaza for water. When James Bowie became seriously ill and was brought to the low barracks where the women might look after him, Ana nursed him as well as she could. It was sad to see such a strong man lie so helpless in fever. Enrique later said that at times Juana Navarro came over from her refuge in the officers' quarters to help.

During a brief truce with the Mexicans when several of the *bejareño* families left the Alamo, Enrique remembered his father's asking Ana if she, too, wanted to leave while she could still take their children to safety. Ana steadfastly replied, "No, if you are going to stay, so am I. If they kill one, they can kill us all."

Life in the Alamo followed an uncertain routine as Mexican artillery shells dropped into the plaza or pounded into the walls of the buildings. Each day Mexican lines and cannon pulled closer around the Alamo in an inescapable encirclement. Voices from the Mexican camps became close enough to understand the words, and their music haunted the Alamo sentinels at night. Spirits rose when the thirty-two Gonzales men rushed through the opened gate to join the defenders.

Everyone believed help would arrive; hope filled the hours of their days and their dreams at night. Someone was always looking toward the horizon for the dust of men marching up the Gonzales or Goliad roads. Within a few days, however, Santa Anna had sealed all the routes toward the Alamo. Ana prayed constantly, fearful for her children and for the fate of her husband at his post on the unprotected east side of the church.

In the early morning darkness of March 6 an incredible blast of cannon fire shook them all awake, and the Alamo men grabbed their rifles to meet the Mexicans pouring into the plaza from all sides. They fought with a desperate cycle of load and fire, load and fire, aiming blindly at the surging Mexican troops, seeing clearly only in the moments when cannon blasts lit the battle scenes. Waves of Mexican soldiers overran the Texans and *tejanos* as they fought hopelessly for their lives.

Soon the Alamo men lay dead, sprawled against the walls or lying in the open, and the Mexican soldiers began the search for any man left alive. Several of the attackers burst into the room where the women were, in pursuit of Brigido Guerrero who fell on his knees, desperately hiding in Ana's skirt. As the Mexicans dragged him out he begged for mercy. He was a captive, he cried, brought into the Alamo and held prisoner. He insisted over and over that he had tried to escape to Santa Anna's forces, but he could not get away. An officer, believing him, pulled him up, "Yes, you can go free." Years later Guerrero received a pension for his service with the Texas Army in 1835.

Several soldiers rushed into the room and, pointing a bayonet at Ana, one demanded, "Where is the money the Americans had?"

"If they had any," she replied, "you may look for it."

An officer's authoritative voice stopped the men, "What are you doing?" he demanded. "You know the women and children are not to be hurt!"

He looked around at the fragile company—Ana and her children, Mrs. Dickinson and her baby, Concepción

Fall of the Alamo by Theodore Gentilz. The French artist, who came to Texas in the mid-1840s, was fascinated by the growing legend of the Alamo. Courtesy Daughters of the Republic of Texas Library at the Alamo.

Losoya and her two children, and other women and children who had sought refuge in the corner room of the church.

"Get your possessions—you have nothing to fear." He directed them out of their little room, into the light of morning. Walking was slow and frightening across the bitter scene. Ana herded María and the boys ahead of her, pushing them around the dead lying in undignified muster. María and Enrique understood—not one valiant *tejano*, not one brave Texan was left alive. The air was heavy, wreathed in grey smoke and the sharp smell of gunpowder—no spiced incense nor rich scent of candle wax to honor these dead. Only thirteen days earlier Gregorio had led his family into the Alamo's shelter and protection. Now tears burned Ana's eyes, but she dared not cry before the children.

"Go to the house of Don Ramón Músquiz," their guard directed. The way was crowded with soldiers and scattered with bricks and stones shot away from the walls of the houses. The office of the political chief of Béxar was a familiar place—Ana and Gregorio had often visited the Músquiz family in happier times. This day, however, their arrival was not a social call and was described by Enrique.

> At about 8 o'clock we became very hungry, up to then not having been given any food. My mother, being familiar with the premises, began to look about for food for herself and children as well as for her other comrades. While she was doing so, Músquiz told her that it was dangerous for her to be moving about and leaving the place and the room in which she was under guard. She told him she did not care whether she was under guard or not, she was going to have something to eat for herself, her children, and her companions whom she intended to feed, if Santa Anna did not feed his prisoners. Músquiz admonished her to silence and told her to be patient and he would get them some food from his own store.

After urging my mother not to leave the room, Músquiz disappeared and went to his pantry, where he got quite a quantity of provisions and brought them to the room in which the prisoners, some ten or a dozen in number, were and distributed the food among them. There was some coffee as well as bread and meat. I recollect that I ate heartily, but my mother ate sparingly.

The next day brought another directive—Santa Anna would meet the women of the Alamo. "What can I say to this man? How can I mask my fear and hatred of him?", Ana thought as she guided the children across Main Plaza. In the presence of Santa Anna the little boys hid in their mother's skirt and María trembled beside her, but Enrique stood away from them by himself. He stared at this man, commander of the soldiers who had killed his father.

The dictator's questions were short, for he already knew what Ana would say. "What is your name, *Señora*?"

"Ana Salazar, *señor*," she replied tersely.

"Not Esparza, *señora*?"

"Si, *señor*, it is Esparza." Ana knew she must speak the truth.

"And your husband, where is he?"

"He lies dead in the Alamo, *señor*."

The dictator asked for names of other members of the Esparza family, and Ana replied that her husband's brother was in the Mexican army. She was not yet aware that Santa Anna had already granted Francisco Esparza permission to search among the Alamo dead for his brother Gregorio's body, to bury it in the *campo santo* among his Esparza kin.

The interview over, an aide handed Ana a *serape*, and two *pesos* from a stack of silver money. She turned away and walked outside to search for a place to stay until she could find a real home for her family. Enrique recalled that a cousin took them into her house for a time. Here María untied the picture of the Virgin from around her neck and hung it on the wall, once again to watch over the family. Enrique also remembered seeing Ana weep during the day, and that he awoke to her sobs at night.

By summertime the Texans and *tejanos* had reclaimed Texas from the defeated Mexicans, and in November the *bejareños* once again gathered in the *campo santo* to decorate the graves with fat blooms of orange and yellow marigolds and to pray for the souls of those buried there.

Ana had hoped that she and her children would be able to return to the old ways in their old home among their friends and neighbors. Her husband was dead and Ana was again a widow, but somehow the family earned enough money for their simple needs—pumpkin and bean seeds for the garden plot beside the *acequia* and pennies for candles to light in honor of the Virgin at San Fernando.

It soon became evident that the poorer and even the prominent *bejareños* of Béxar would suffer from the "straggling American adventurers" who coveted and soon came to own not only their ranch lands but even old homesteads clustered about the plazas. Despite all of the changes, Ana was able to keep her family together until the boys were old enough to work on farms around Béxar. She died on the feast day of Guadalupe, the twelfth of December in 1847, and María followed her in May of 1849. They did not live to benefit from Gregorio's legacy of land which Enrique and his two brothers received from the state of Texas as the heirs of an Alamo hero.

The thirteen days she endured in the Alamo earned Ana a prominent place among Texas' heroines as a participant in the siege of the Alamo and as a witness to the glory of the courage displayed there.

Enrique Esparza. The accounts of the retired farmer, of his experiences as a young boy, enriched the legend and lore of the Alamo. Courtesy the Adina de Zavala Papers, The Center for American History of the University of Texas at Austin.

ENRIQUE ESPARZA

Son of Brave *Tejanos*

❧

Enrique Esparza was among many young boys playing on Military Plaza that wintry afternoon of February 23, 1836, yet he was the only one of them who later publicly recounted his experiences on that day in San Antonio de Béxar. He waited almost seventy years before talking openly about that frightful time, but in the early 1900s several of his interviews appeared in the San Antonio *Daily Express*. Some of his recollections had been clouded by the long intervening years, but a thread of authenticity runs throughout. Although he was a respected citizen of San Antonio, it appears that, before his interviews, only his family had known about his experiences during the siege and final storming of the Alamo when his father died with the other brave defenders fighting for the Texas cause against the Mexican government. Perhaps Enrique, as an old man, finally began to talk openly of his experiences in the Alamo because, with none of the defenders left alive after the battle, he wanted to tell his account before he, too, died.

His story begins in a simple fashion.

> I was born in one of the old adobe houses that formerly stood on the east side of what we call *Calle de Acequia* or the street of the ditch, but now known as Main Avenue. The house was but a short distance north of Salinas Street. I am the son of Gregorio Esparza.

On February 23 Enrique glimpsed a scene he never forgot. "I saw Santa Anna, when he arrived. I saw him dismount. He did not hitch his horse to an iron ring on the Governor's Palace as some later said. Instead he pitched the bridle reins to a sentry."

Enrique had already known for weeks about the powerful dictator of Mexico and Texas, from the endless talk among the *bejareños* of his cruelties. Santa Anna as a young military cadet had fought in the Battle of Medina with the victorious Royalist forces which had crushed a rebellion against Spain and gained control of nearby Béxar. Here the young officer spent the next few months contracting debts he never paid and trying unsuccessfully to arrange a marriage with a young girl of the Navarro family. By the time the Spanish withdrew, Santa Anna had established an unsavory reputation and left few friends in the provincial outpost.

But that was over twenty years ago, and today Santa Anna was back. Enrique ran to his home, not far from Main Plaza, where family friend John W. Smith had just arrived with the warning. If the Esparzas' plans had worked out, by this time the family would have been well along the road to Gonzales, away from battle's dangers. But the wagon had not come for them. For days *bejareños* had been in a high state of nervousness, fearing the approaching Mexican army, and even before dawn that morning the Esparzas had heard their neighbors loading carts with household goods for safety in the country.

Enrique's father Gregorio had heard the shocking report of the entrance of the Mexican army into Béxar and had already rushed home, deciding his family's only safety was in the Alamo with him. Ana met him at the door and listened to his urgent message. María hurried to help her mother. Enrique and his father carried the food and household goods as they all followed Gregorio out of the house. In Enrique's memory the time was the hour before sunset as they hurried from their home heading up the hill toward the Alamo. "It was pitch dark soon afterward," he remembered. Behind them Mexican troops thronged the narrow streets of Béxar, and Enrique heard the roll of Mexican military drums from the plazas as they scrambled across the irrigation ditch just west of the Alamo plaza walls, in which "all the doors were closed and barred. I remember the main entrance was on the south side of the large enclosure." In a desperate scramble they pushed their way inside through the small opening near the main gate. "The sentinels that had been on duty without were first called inside, and then the openings had been closed. Some sentinels were posted upon the roof, but these were protected by the walls of the Alamo church and the old Convent building."

The boy recalled that, "The quarters [for the soldiers] were not in the church but on the south side of the fort, on either side of the entrance and [others] were part of the convent." The family followed Gregorio to the church and Enrique recalled "it was shut up, when we arrived. The window was opened to permit us to enter." Gregorio leaped inside, then María lifted her two brothers to his waiting hands and scrambled up after them. Enrique followed, then Ana climbed in last, once the children were safe. For a moment they stood gasping for breath—looking at each other. They were safe! They were all together!

> I distinctly remember that I climbed through the window, and over cannon that was placed inside the church immediately behind the window. There were several other cannon there. Some were back of the doors. Some had been mounted on the roof and some had been placed in the Convent.

The window was closed immediately after the family was inside, and here they remained during the twelve days of siege. Enrique recalled other refugee families in the Alamo—James Bowie's sister-in-law Juana Navarro Alsbury and her sister Gertrudis. There was a "family of several girls, two of whom [he] knew afterwards." He saw Concepción Losoya and her son Juan, who was a little older than he, and had a vivid memory of a woman's "making circles on the ground with her umbrella. I had seen very few umbrellas," he admitted. During the night the children slept restlessly in the drafts of the church, and Enrique awoke to the sentry calls of the night patrol. He sensed the dangers of his father's life as he watched Gregorio run up the high ramp in the church to his post under the open sky. Through the cold February and March nights the gunners slept fitfully alongside their guns, often awakening to glance up at the stars of Orion to see what time it was.

In one of his first interviews, but not repeated in later interviews, Enrique recalled that:

> On the first night a company of which my father was one went out and captured some prisoners. One of them was a Mexican soldier, and all through the siege he interpreted the bugle calls on the Mexican side, and in this way the Americans kept posted on the movements of the enemy.

At the beginning of the siege "there was a ditch of running water in back of the church, to the east, and another on the west side of Alamo plaza. We couldn't get to the ditch as it was under fire and the other one Santa Anna cut off." The next morning, "after we had gotten in the fort I saw the men drawing water from a well in the convent yard. The well was located a little south of the center of the square. I do not know if it is still there or not," he observed. The well was the main source of water for all the inhabitants of the Alamo, yet to go out in the plaza to draw up water was to risk being fired upon by enemy sharpshooters.

Enrique recalled his family had not been in the Alamo long:

> When a messenger came from Santa Anna calling on us to surrender. I remember the reply at this summons was a shot fired from one of the cannon on the roof of the Alamo. Soon after it was fired, I heard Santa Anna's cannon reply.

The frightened women and children could hear the

Mexican "cannon strike the walls of the church where they were, and also the convent." Enrique vividly remembered the answering sounds as "the cannon within the Alamo buildings, both church and convent, fired repeatedly during the night." He heard the "cheers of the Alamo gunners and the deriding jeers of Santa Anna's troops."

In a short armistice "of three days" a close friend of Enrique's father brought news that:

> Santa Anna had offered to let the Americans go with their lives if they would surrender, but the Mexicans would be treated as rebels. During this armistice my father told my mother she had better take the children and go, while she could do so safely. But my mother refused to leave.

The only person Enrique remembered who left the Alamo was a beautiful young girl named Trinidad Saucedo.

Young Enrique shared in the hope that extra troops would arrive to help the Alamo men. "After a few days I remember that a messenger came from somewhere with word that help was coming. The Americans celebrated it by beating drums and playing on the flute." On another night, however, "there was music in the Mexican camp, and when the music grew louder we knew it meant that [Mexican] reinforcements had arrived." At about the same time news came to the Alamo, brought by a "messenger who got through the lines saying that communication had been cut off and the promised reinforcements could not be sent."

During the days of the siege, Enrique watched the Alamo soldiers firing toward the enemy and thought that:

> If I had been given a weapon, I would have fought likewise. But weapons and ammunitions were scarce and only wielded and used by those who knew how. But I saw some there no older than I who had them and fought as bravely, and died as stolidly as the adults.

For Enrique the days were long and full of terror, and the nights even longer and fraught with still more fear. Among the soldiers he remembered quite well was the legendary David Crockett, who for some reason he called "Don Benito." The tall Kentucky hero would often stop by the family's little campfire to warm his hands and would say a few words to the children "in the Mexican language." In his first interview Enrique stated that he remembered "hearing the names of Travis and Bowie mentioned, but never saw either of them." Only in later interviews did he describe in detail Travis' drawing the line for his men to cross. He recounted James Bowie's last heroic moments, which could not have been visible to the women and children hidden away in the church.

Yet Enrique did witness actual heroism and experience frightening scenes during the final attack by the Mexican army on March 6. It began "about 2 o'clock in the morning. There was a great shouting and firing at the northwest corner of the fort." Enrique saw his father one last time as he "went into the fight" at the cannon station above the church.

Enrique's description of the final assault on the Alamo remains graphic and powerful in its simplicity. He spoke of the battle in the proud terms of a loyal *tejano,* the son of an Alamo hero.

> The end came suddenly and almost unexpectedly and with a rush. It came at night and when all was dark save when there was a gleam of fire from the flash and flame of a fired gun.
>
> Our men had fought hard the day before. Their ammunition was very low. That of many was entirely spent. Santa Anna must have known this for his men were able to make several breeches in the walls. Our men had fought long and hard and well. But their strength was spent. Many slept. Few there were who were awake. Even those on guard beside the breeches dozed.
>
> The fire from the Mexicans had slacked and finally ceased. Those who were awake saw the

Mexicans lying quietly by their camp fires and thought they likewise slept. But our foes were only simulating sleep, or if they slept, were awakened by their savage chief and his brutal officers.

After all had been dark and quiet for many hours and I had fallen into a profound slumber suddenly there was a terrible din. Cannon boomed. Their shot crashed through the doors and windows and the breeches in the walls. Then men rushed in on us. They fired on us in vollies. They struck us down with their *escopetas*. In the dark our men groped and grasped the throats of our foes and buried their knives in their hearts.

As the fierce fighting continued in the darkness, "we could hear the Mexican officers shouting to the men to jump over" the walls. "Men were fighting so close that we could hear them strike each other," he recalled. "It was so dark we couldn't see anything, and the families that were in the quarters just huddled up in the corners. My mother's children were near her."

Mexican troops filled the plaza, spilling into the church. "Finally they began shooting through the dark into the room where we were." Enrique guessed they "fired into the room for at least fifteen minutes. It was a miracle, but none of the children were touched." Enrique recorded the singular heroism of an unnamed, Texas boy who was staying with the families.

By my side was an American boy. He was about my own age but larger. As they approached us, he rose to his feet. He had been sleeping, but like myself, he had been rudely awakened. As they rushed upon him he stood calmly and across his shoulders drew the blanket on which he had slept. He was unarmed. They slew him where he stood and his corpse fell over me.

"By daybreak the firing had almost stopped, and through the window we could see shadows of men moving around inside the fort." The Mexicans went from room to room looking for an American to kill. Soldiers entered the room where the women and children were, but an officer stepped in and ordered them to leave. He directed Ana to "pick out her own family and get her baggage." The other women followed the same instructions. Fearfully the refugees made their way slowly through the battle-wrecked Alamo Plaza. Walking carefully they marveled at the still bodies of the fallen men, their bearded faces darkened with burned gunpowder.

Outside Enrique saw no one he knew. Mexican soldiers crowded their passage down to Presa Street. These were fresh troops "who did not fire a shot during the battle," he observed. "Santa Anna had many more troops than he could use." Enrique went with his family to Ramón Músquiz's home to wait until they would be summoned to meet with Santa Anna.

The women captives had their interviews the next day. Enrique recalled that Juana Navarro Alsbury and her sister Gertrudis Navarro were interviewed first and released to their father, the loyal Mexican supporter José Ángel Navarro. Mrs. Susanna Dickinson with her baby Angelina followed them.

"My mother was next called before the dictator," he remembered. Once inside Santa Anna's headquarters, Enrique's brothers pressed close to their mother, but he "stood to one side and behind her" watching every move and listening to the words that passed between his brave mother and the stern dictator. He first asked Ana her name, which she gave. "Where is your husband?" No one had spoken to her of Gregorio until now. Quietly she answered, "He is dead in the Alamo."

Santa Anna ordered an aide to hand Ana two silver *pesos* and a *serape* and dismissed her in the same disinterested manner he ended all his interviews with the women. She found a place in Béxar for her family to live, and Enrique soon walked out among the Mexican soldiers in the plazas. Dodging the men on horseback, he stalked the dictator, running among the crowds looking for him.

I went to Main Plaza and watched the soldiers of Santa Anna and saw him quite a number of times before they marched away towards Houston, where he was defeated. He had a hard and cruel look and his countenance was a very sinister one. It has haunted me ever since I last saw it. I will never forget the face or the figure of Santa Anna.

Enrique Esparza and his brothers survived the horrifying battle, grew up and secured lands which the Republic of Texas gave to the heirs of the Alamo heroes. For many years Enrique farmed in Atascosa County. As an old man he lived with a son in Losoya, where he lies buried in the cemetery beside the church. On All Soul's Day, flowers decorate his grave to honor the boy who remembered his *tejano* parents, Gregorio and Ana Esparza, and his own childhood days and nights during the siege and storming of the Alamo.

Detail from Stephen F. Austin's 1836 Map of Texas by H.S. Tanner

EPILOGUE

ॐ

Few military conflicts in American history have created as much interest among historical writers, artists, and movie makers as the siege and fall of the Alamo. None of the women and children who survived within the fortress-church wrote of their experiences, and their verbal memories of the battle, as recorded by journalist interviewers, were later questioned and often interpreted. Both Juana Navarro Pérez Alsbury and Madame Candelaria related their experiences in the Alamo only to have their memories questioned as being faulty. Susanna Dickinson was confronted with inaccurate reports concerning her husband's death.

Susanna became a self-declared authority on the battle of the Alamo and at times spoke with bias. Although she never personally talked with Juana Alsbury after the battle, she discredited Juana's experiences and even branded her a traitor to the Texas cause, perhaps because Juana was a woman of Mexican descent married to a Texan, Horatio Alsbury, who was in the Alamo during the first days of the siege but who was sent out as a messenger before the final attack. Susanna recalled that as the Mexican army entered Béxar, "Dr. Alsbury retreated to the Alamo with his Mexican wife and sister-in-law." She did not see him leave. Enrique Esparza, who recounted his experiences in 1907, over seventy years after the fall of the Alamo, recalled, "William [John W.] Smith and Dr. Alsbury were among those who were sent for help" from the Alamo. John S. Ford quoted Juana as expecting her husband to return to the Alamo.

Enrique Esparza's recollection that the ill Bowie "was

placed in one of the smaller rooms on the north side of the church [and] Mrs. Alsbury and my mother were among those who nursed him and ministered to his wants," contradicts Juana's story that she saw Bowie few times after he left the officers' quarters. Esparza insisted that she "was near Bowie when he was killed," adding that for safety the women and children fled "to Bowie's room, when the soldiers entered the old church." Juana, in her account, tells of being in the officers' quarters during the final storming.

Conflicting accounts cloud the exact location of the ill Bowie at the time of his death at the hands of Mexican soldiers. Had he been moved to the old *convento* or long barracks-turned-hospital and there placed in the southwest room in the second story? Or had he remained in the south section, the "gambler's den," where he was moved after he developed typhoid fever and where Candelaria had gone to nurse him? Dr. John Sutherland in his sketch of the Alamo some years later placed Bowie in his original location in the officers' quarters on the northwest side of the Alamo Plaza. According to Enrique Esparza's recollection, Bowie was finally moved into the safety of the church near the women and children where they might look after him. The tangle of the contradictory accounts remains to this day.

One of the most persistent questions raised against Juana was whether or not she was actually still in the fortress during the final battle. In one interview Susanna insisted that Ángel Navarro had "personally escorted his daughters" away from the Alamo during the early parleys between the warring factions. As late as 1893 a kinswoman of Horatio Alsbury revived the reports of Juana's desertion, alleging that "Mrs. Juana Navarro Alsbury, the Doctor's wife, was in the Alamo until the day before the fort was stormed by the Mexicans, when she was taken out by Santa Anna under a flag of truce at the request of her father Don Juan [Ángel] Navarro." By Esparza's eyewitness account, however, the Navarro sisters "stayed in the Alamo until it fell. They feared to leave," he commented, "believing the Mexicans under Santa Anna would kill them."

Several supposedly unbiased reports from Mexican sources indicate that one of the women in the Alamo was less-than-loyal to the Texan cause. Santa Anna's secretary noted that about nightfall of the fifth of March Travis, "through the intermediary of a woman, proposed to the [Mexican] general-in-chief to surrender arms and fort and everybody in it in exchange for saving his own life and that of all his comrades in arms." Susanna claimed that Juana was the woman messenger and that, while in the Mexican camp, betrayed the situation in the Alamo, revealing the number of men as well as their weakened condition. Another Mexican source reported that Travis had promised his men that if reinforcements did not arrive by March 5, they would either surrender or try to escape the next day. This information was given the Mexicans "by a lady from Béxar." Neither Mexican source, however, indicated that the woman was Juana, although her prominent name was known among the Mexican command.

Susanna Dickinson was confronted with an erroneous report concerning the death of her husband Almaron. Soon after the battle, word spread from the Mexican forces that a Texas soldier had jumped from the artillery post on the east side of the Alamo church with a young boy in his arms, and that Mexican soldiers had felled the two with bullets. The reports identified the Texan as Almaron Dickinson, but their identification was incorrect—Dickinson had an infant daughter. Sam Houston, in Gonzales five days after the Alamo battle, also circulated the same incorrect information in a letter to Fannin in Goliad, "Lieutenant Dickinson, who had a wife and child in the fort, after having fought with desperate courage, tied his child to his back, leaped from the top of a two story building, and both were killed by the fall." Gunner Anthony Wolfe, stationed with Dickinson at the artillery post, did have a young son who was not listed among the Alamo dead nor among the women and children who survived. It is possible that in the final moments of battle, Wolfe grabbed his younger son and jumped from the Alamo walls. Enrique Esparza reported that a brave young Texan, possibly Anthony Wolfe's other son, was shot by the Mexicans when, unarmed, he bravely confronted them. Susanna's version of the fate of the Wolfe family asserted that when Anthony escaped the first attack he begged for mercy from the Mexicans. "He was instantly killed." Of his two sons, she reported, "the little fellows came to my room where the Mexicans killed them."

To further muddle the Dickinson-Wolfe legend, artist Theodore Gentilz came to San Antonio about 1848 and talked with old San Antonio residents, listening to their various recollections of the Alamo battle. For his painting "Death of Dickinson" the artist discarded the versions which claimed that Lieutenant Dickinson "with a child on his back leaped from an upper window in the east end of the church, but their lifeless bodies fell to the ground riddled with bullets." The artist instead chose a second version to illustrate his "Death of Dickinson," and his painting shows a man outside the Alamo kneeling with a young boy as he pleads for their lives before Santa Anna. Even though Gentilz has the reputation for thorough research in preparation for his historical works, in this case the power of drama seems to have overcome his usual attention to more accepted historical evidence.

Perhaps one of the most intriguing of the Alamo legends is the presence of the two Wolfe brothers in the Alamo and of their deaths during the battle. They had arrived in Béxar with their father Anthony Wolfe in James G. Swisher's Company. Records reveal that Wolfe fell ill at Washington-on-the-Brazos and, after his recovery several weeks later, joined Swisher's Washington Company enroute to San Antonio de Béxar. Anthony Wolfe's name appears on muster rolls of citizen-volunteers of both the siege and storming of Béxar in late 1835 and on those of the Alamo volunteers. Since the two boys were dependents, their names are not listed alongside their father's. Thomas Jefferson Rusk later wrote that, fighting beside the men of Swisher's Company during the Grass Fight on Alazon Creek, was a boy with a gun who survived a

The Death of Dickinson. Artist Theodore Gentilz chose a widely circulated but false legend for his depiction of the death of Almaron Dickinson. Courtesy Daughters of the Republic of Texas Library at the Alamo.

powerful Mexican artillery blast. Perhaps he was Wolfe's eldest son joining his father in the sharp confrontation.

In 1841 Anthony Wolfe's widow, Mary Victoria Durst Wolfe Tausin of Nacogdoches, applied for the land due Wolfe for his military service and for his death in the Alamo. In her petition she made no mention of the two boys although she and Anthony are listed as having a son. In some judgments, however, the Wolfe boys' presence is indeed accounted for, and they retain their identity in history through the memories which others had of them in Béxar and in the Alamo.

Through the years Susanna spoke as if she had witnessed the deaths of Travis, Bowie, and Crockett. Since she was hidden within the small church room, she could not have seen them die. After she left the Alamo, however, and while she was still in San Antonio, accounts of the three heroes' deaths were told and retold by the victorious Mexicans. The Ramón Músquiz family surely knew of the reports and told Susanna. In time she recounted these incidents in her own stories as if she had witnessed them. Although she knew these men and visited with them, she did not see them die.

Joe, Travis' black slave and aide-de-camp, gave his eye-witness account of the Alamo commander's death. He asserted that Travis, after being shot in the head, remained alive long enough to kill the officer who sought to run him through with a sword.

Esparza described in detail Travis' drawing the immortal north-south line, an event which he might possibly have seen. The probability of witnessing James Bowie's death is less likely. The hero's final minutes occurred during the violent fighting and was not visible to the women and children hidden in the church room. Perhaps the old man's interviewer added the mythical story to make the boy's experiences even more exciting.

Madame Candelaria told and retold her Alamo experiences in the half-century following the battle. During her lifetime many of the Béxar residents who knew her personally believed what she said. Juana Alsbury, recalling those anxious days and nights of the siege, did not rule out Candelaria's claim to being one of Jim Bowie's nurses. "There were people in the Alamo I did not see," she generously admitted.

Disbelievers, insisting Madame Candelaria was not present during the battle, discredit her remembrances as an eyewitness to the events she described. Lon Tinkle in his *13 Days to Glory* regarded Madame Candelaria's accounts as "self-contradictory." Several years later Walter Lord in his definitive work on the Alamo, *A Time to Stand,* concluded that Madame Candelaria—"one of the better-known claimants—definitely was not in the Alamo." Yet they offer little evidence to prove her wrong. Through the decades Candelaria never waivered in her recollections of the events she claimed to have witnessed. One elderly *bejareño* who knew her remarked, "She is old, maybe a hundred. She might have been in the Alamo during the fight. *Quien sabe?*"

The Alamo's epic tale has been recounted by many story tellers. Each remembrance, however fragile, was woven into a tapestry of innumerable threads of truth and fantasy, reality and imagination. Which are and which are not pure imagination? *Quien sabe?*

Bibliography

History of the Alamo

MANUSCRIPTS AND DOCUMENTS

Alamo. Files. Daughters of the Republic of Texas Library at the Alamo.

Alamo Scrapbook. The Center for American History , University of Texas at Austin.

Battle of the Alamo. Files. Daughters of the Republic of Texas Library at the Alamo.

Crimmins, M. L. Collection. "The Alamo." Daughters of the Republic of Texas Library at the Alamo.

De Zavala, Adina. Collection. "Alamo Mission Research." The Center for American History, University of Texas at Austin.

Gentilz, Theodore. Collection, Box SM-2. Daughters of the Republic of Texas Library at the Alamo.

Potter, Reuben. Letter to Henry McArdle, August 15, 1874. Henry McArdle, "Dawn at the Alamo." Scrapbook, vol. 1. Archives Division, Texas State Library.

Swisher, J. G., Captain, Company. "List of men who have this day volunteered to remain before Béxar," November 24, 1835. The Center for American History, University of Texas at Austin.

PRINTED MATERIAL

Ahlborn, Richard Eighme. *The San Antonio Missions: Edward Everett and the American Occupation, 1847.* Fort Worth: Amon Carter Museum, 1985.

Chabot, Frederick C. *The Alamo. Mission, Fortress and Shrine.* San Antonio, 1935.

Corner, William, comp. "Some Further Notes on the Alamo." *San Antonio de Béxar.* San Antonio, 1890.

De la Peña, José Enrique. *With Santa Anna in Texas: A Personal Narrative of the Revolution.* Carmen Perry (trans. and ed.). College Station: Texas A & M University Press, 1975.

De Zavala, Adina. *History of the Alamo and Other Missions in San Antonio.* San Antonio, 1917.

Gould, Stephen. "The Historic Alamo and Grenet Business Emporium. A Bonanza For Sale." *Alamo City Guide.* San Antonio: n.p., 1882.

Gray, William F. *From Virginia to Texas, 1835.* 1909. Reprint. Houston: Fletcher Young Publishing Co., 1965.

Groneman, Bill. *Alamo Defenders.* Austin: Eakin Press, 1990.

Houston, Sam. Letter to James W. Fannin, Gonzales, March 11, 1836. *The Papers of the Texas Revolution, 1835-1836.* Vol. 5. John H. Jenkins (gen. ed.). Austin: Presidial Press, 1973.

Hunter, J. Marvin, ed. "Survived the Alamo Massacre." *Frontier Times* vol. 6 (April, 1929).

Lord, Walter. A *Time To Stand.* New York: Harper & Brothers, 1961.

_____. "Myths & Realities of the Alamo." *The Republic of Texas.* Stephen B. Oates (gen. ed.). Palo Alto, California: American West Publishing Company, 1968.

Lozano, Ruben Rendon. *Viva Tejas. The Story of The Tejanos, The Mexican-born Patriots of the Texas Revolution.* 1936. Reprint. Mary Ann Noonan Guerra. San Antonio: Alamo Press, 1985.

Miller, Thomas Lloyd. *Bounty And Donation Land Grants of Texas, 1835-1888.* Austin: University of Texas Press, 1967.

Myers, John Myers. *The Alamo.* New York: E. P. Dutton and Company, Inc., 1948.

Ruíz, Francisco Antonio. "Fall of the Alamo, and Massacre of Travis and His Brave Associates," J. A. Quintero (trans.). *Texas Almanac for 1860.* Dallas: A. H. Belo, 1860.

Rusk, Thomas J. "Account of the Grass Fight." *The Papers of Mirabeau Buonaparte Lamar.* Vol. 3. Charles Adams Gulick, Jr., and Katherine Elliott (eds.), c. 1920. Reprint. Austin: Pemberton Press, 1968.

Schoelwer, Susan Prendergast. "The Artist's Alamo: A Reappraisal of Pictorial Evidence, 1836-1850." *Southwestern Historical Quarterly.* Vol. 91 (April, 1988).

_____, with Tom W. Gläser. *Alamo Images, Changing Perceptions Of A Texas Experience.* Dallas: DeGolyer Library and Southern Methodist University Press, 1985.

Steinbomer, Dorothy Kendall and Carmen Perry. *Gentilz: Artist Of The Old Southwest, Drawings and Paintings by Theodore Gentilz.* Austin: University of Texas Press, 1974.

The Alamo Long Barracks Museum. Daughters of the Republic of Texas. San Antonio, 1986.

Williams, Amelia. "A Critical Study Of The Siege Of The Alamo And Of The Personnel Of Its Defenders," *Southwestern Historical Quarterly.* Vol. 37 (January, 1934).

_____. "Texas Collection." *Southwestern Historical Quarterly.* Vol. 37 (April, 1946).

Juana Navarro Pérez Alsbury

MANUSCRIPTS AND DOCUMENTS

Alsbury, H. A. File. Daughters of the Republic of Texas Library at the Alamo.

Alsbury, Juana Navarro Pérez. File. Archives Division, Texas State Library.

_____. File. Daughters of the Republic of Texas Library at the Alamo.

Dickinson, Susanna. File. Daughters of the Republic of Texas Library at the Alamo.

Ford, John Salmon. Papers. "Mrs. Alsbury's Recollections Of The Fall of the Alamo." The Center for American History, University of Texas at Austin.

Navarro Family. Papers. Daughters of the Republic of Texas Library at the Alamo.

Navarro, José Angel. Probate papers. Béxar County Clerk. San Antonio.

PRINTED MATERIAL

Barnard, J. H. *Dr. J. H. Barnard's Journal.* 1912. Reprint. Goliad: 1965.

Barciñas, Andres and Ansolma Bergara. Deposition. Gonzales, March 11, 1836. *The Papers of the Texas Revolution, 1835-1836.* Vol. 5, John H. Jenkins (gen. ed.). Austin: Presidial Press, 1973.

Menchaca, Antonio. *Memoirs.* San Antonio: Yanaguana Society, 1937.

Maverick, Mary Adams. *Memoirs of Mary A. Maverick.* Edited by Rena Maverick Green. San Antonio: 1921.

Madame Candelaria

MANUSCRIPTS AND DOCUMENTS

Cameron, Minnie B. "Vernon Moore White." In "Artists and Musicians of Texas, 1924-1926" (typescript). San Antonio Public Library, San Antonio.

McArdle, H. A. Letter. October 21, 1901. Garrison Papers. The Center for American History, University of Texas at Austin.

Madame Candelaria. Files. Archives Division, Texas State Library.

_____. Files. Daughters of the Republic of Texas Library at the Alamo.

PRINTED MATERIAL

Creel, George. "Glorious Defeat." *Collier's* 84 (July 6, 1929).

Cresens, Johnnie. "Early Texas Artists Featured in Exhibit." Austin *American,* April 16, 1953.

Elfer, Maurice. *Madam Candelaria.* Houston: The Rein Company Publishers, 1933.

Lanier, Sidney. "San Antonio de Béxar." In *San Antonio de Béxar.* William Corner (comp. and ed.). San Antonio, 1890.

"The Last Voice Hushed." San Antonio *Daily Express,* February 11,1899.

Voss, Frederick S. "Portraying an American Original: The

Likenesses of Davy Crockett." *Southwestern Historical Quarterly*, vol. XCI, April, 1988.

Waugh, Julia Nott. *Castro-Ville and Henry Castro, Empresario.* San Antonio: Standard Printing Company, 1934.

Susanna Dickinson

DOCUMENTS AND MANSCRIPTS

Bellows, Susanna. Memorial. Third Texas Legislature, November 9, 1849. Folder 7, Class RG, Box 100-367. Archives Division, Texas State Library.

Dickinson, Susanna. "To the Honorable House of Representatives of the Republic of Texas." Columbia, October 16th, 1836. Archives Division, Texas State Library.

Dickinson, Almeron. File. Daughters of the Republic of Texas Library at the Alamo.

PRINTED MATERIALS

Callihan, Elmer. L. "Later Romantic Years of Mrs. Dickinson." Dallas *Morning News*, March 9, 1936.

Fields, W (comp.). *The Scrap-Book.* Philadelphia: Edward Meeks, 1890.

Houston, Sam. Letter to James W. Fannin, Gonzales, March 11, 1836. *The Papers of the Texas Revolution, 1835-1836*, vol 3. John H. Jenkins (gen. ed.). Austin: Presidial Press, 1973.

_____. Letter to James Collingsworth, Camp at Navidad, March 15, 1836. *The Papers of the Texas Revolution, 1835-1836*, vol. 3. John H. Jenkins (gen. ed.). Austin: Presidial Press, 1973.

King, C. Richard. *Susanna Dickinson.* Austin: Shoal Creek Publishers, Inc., 1976.

Morris, Mrs. Harry Joseph., comp. and ed. *Founders and Patriots of the Republic of Texas.* Vol. 1. N.p.: The Daughters of the Republic of Texas, 1963.

Zuber, William Physick. *My Eighty Years In Texas.* Austin: University of Texas Press, 1971.

Concepción Charlí Gortari Losoya

MANUSCRIPTS AND DOCUMENTS

Charlí, Concepción. Losoya Files. Daughters of the Republic of Texas Library at the Alamo.

Losoya. Files. Daughters of the Republic of Texas Library at the Alamo

Losoya, Miguel. Land, Acquisition and Consfication. Parks—Travis. Clipping File. Daughters of the Republic of Texas Library at the Alamo.

Mission Records. Distribution of Mission de Valero Lands to Refugees from Los Adaes. Béxar Archives. Daughters of the Republic of Texas Library at the Alamo.

Villanueva, Candelario. Deposition [Remembering Toribio Losoya], 1837. Daughters of the Republic Library at the Alamo.

PRINTED MATERIALS

Barnes, C. M. "Famous Old Families." San Antonio *Daily Express*, December 16, 1907.

Jackson, Jack. *Los Mesteños, Spanish Ranching in Texas, 1721-1821*. College Station: Texas A & M University Press, 1986.

Lewis, Mark. "Remembering the Alamo." San Antonio *Light*, May 10,1992.

Todd, Betsy Palmer. *Losoya. An Unsung Hero Of the Alamo*. Golden, Colorado: Adolph Coors Brewing Company, 1986.

Ana Salazar de Esparza

MANUSCRIPTS AND DOCUMENTS

DeShields, James Thomas. Papers. "Battle of Béxar." Daughters of the Republic of Texas Library at the Alamo.

Esparza. Files. Daughters of the Republic of Texas Library at the Alamo.

Esparza, Francisco. Deposition [Remembering Gregorio Esparza, his brother], 1859. Alamo Curator's Library at the Alamo.

Esparza, Gregoria *[sic]*. Estate. Probate papers. Bexar County Clerk. San Antonio.

Lefler, James Bradley. Papers, 1870-1967. Daughters of the Republic of Texas Library at the Alamo.

PRINTED MATERIAL

Chabot, Frederick C. *With The Makers of San Antonio.* San Antonio: 1937.

Driggs, Howard R. *Rise of the Lone Star.* New York: Frederick A. Stokes Company, 1936.

Ivey, Jake. "The Problem of the Two Guerreros." *Alamo Lore and Myth Organization.* Vol. 4 (March, 1982).

Miller, Thomas Lloyd. *Bounty And Donation Land Grants Of Texas, 1835-1888.* Austin: University Of Texas Press, 1967.

Enrique Esparza

MANUSCRIPTS AND DOCUMENTS

De Zavala, Adina. Collection. The Center for American History, University of Texas at Austin.

Esparza, Enrique. Deed Records. Bexar County Clerk's Office, San Antonio.

Esparza, Gregorio. File. Bexar County. General Land Office, Austin.

Esparza, Henrique *[sic]*. File. Bexar County. General Land Office, Austin.

Esparza. Files. Daughters of the Republic of Texas Library at the Alamo.

PRINTED MATERIAL

Barnes, Charles Merritt. "Alamo's Only Survivor." San Antonio *Daily Express,* May, 12, 19, 1907.

Hutton, Jim. "Esparza's story colored by legends." San Antonio *Express-News,* June 9, 1991.

"Story of the Massacre of Heroes of the Alamo." San Antonio *Daily Express,* March 7, 1904.

"Last Survivor of Alamo Dead: Saw End of Defenders." San Antonio *Express*, December 21, 1917.